FLANNERY O'CONNOR

Literature and Life series

(Formerly Modern Literature and World Dramatists)

General Editor: Philip Winsor

Selected list of titles:

EDWARD ALBEE, *Ronald Hayman*
JAMES BALDWIN, *Carolyn Wedin Sylvander*
SAUL BELLOW, *Brigitte Scheer-Schäzler*
TRUMAN CAPOTE, *Helen S. Garson*
WILLA CATHER, *Dorothy Tuck McFarland*
JOAN DIDION, *Katherine Usher Henderson*
EARLY AMERICAN DRAMATISTS, *Jack A. Vaughn*
ELLEN GLASGOW, *Marcelle Thiébaux*
LILLIAN HELLMAN, *Doris V. Falk*
JOHN IRVING, *Gabriel Miller*
CHRISTOPHER ISHERWOOD, *Claude J. Summers*
KEN KESEY, *Barry H. Leeds*
ROBERT LOWELL, *Burton Raffel*
MARY McCARTHY, *Willene Schaefer Hardy*
CARSON McCULLERS, *Richard M. Cook*
MARIANNE MOORE, *Elizabeth Phillips*
JOYCE CAROL OATES, *Ellen G. Friedman*
FLANNERY O'CONNOR, *Dorothy Tuck McFarland*
KATHERINE ANNE PORTER, *John Edward Hardy*
PHILIP ROTH, *Judith Jones and Guinevera Nance*
JOHN STEINBECK, *Paul McCarthy*
LIONEL TRILLING, *Edward Joseph Shoben, Jr.*
GORE VIDAL, *Robert F. Kiernan*
EUDORA WELTY, *Elizabeth Evans*
EDITH WHARTON, *Richard H. Lawson*
TENNESSEE WILLIAMS, *Felicia Hardison Londré*

Complete list of titles in the series on request.

FLANNERY O'CONNOR

Dorothy Tuck McFarland

FREDERICK UNGAR PUBLISHING CO.

NEW YORK

Copyright © 1976 by Frederick Ungar Publishing Co., Inc.
Printed in the United States of America
Library of Congress Catalog Card Number: 74-78443
Designed by Anita Duncan
ISBN: 0-8044-2609-0

Library of Congress Cataloging in Publication Data
McFarland, Dorothy Tuck, 1938–
    Flannery O'Connor.
    (Modern literature monographs)
    Bibliography: p.
    Includes index.
    1. O'Connor, Flannery—Criticism and interpretation.
PS3565.C57Z75   813'.5'4   74–78443
ISBN 0–8044–2609–0

Second Printing, 1983

for Lina

If we profess that this is the End of Desire, fewer people than ever will want to experience it.

Charles Williams, *Many Dimensions*

Contents

Chronology   ix

1   Introduction   1

2   *A Good Man Is Hard to Find*   13

3   *Everything That Rises Must Converge*   43

4   *Wise Blood*   73

5   *The Violent Bear It Away*   91

6   Conclusion   113

Notes   117

Bibliography   121

Index   125

Chronology

1925	25 March: Mary Flannery O'Connor is born in Savannah, Georgia, the only child of Regina Cline and Edwin Francis O'Connor.
late 1930's	Mr. O'Connor develops disseminated lupus and the family moves to Milledgeville, Georgia, the home of the Cline family since before the Civil War.
1941	Mr. O'Connor dies.
1945	Mary Flannery graduates from Georgia State College for Women.
1945–47	Attends Iowa State University; drops "Mary" from her name.
1946	Her first story, "The Geranium," published in *Accent*.
1947	Begins first novel, *Wise Blood*.
1947	June: awarded MFA degree from University of Iowa.
1947–48	Lives at Yaddo writers' colony at Saratoga Springs, New York.
1949–50	Lives in New York City and Connecticut, writing.
1950	December: returns to Georgia; stricken with disseminated lupus.
1951	Moves with mother to dairy farm, "Andalusia," five miles from Milledgeville.
1952	*Wise Blood* is published.
1955	*A Good Man Is Hard To Find and Other Stories* published.

1960   *The Violent Bear It Away* published.

1963   Receives honorary degree from Smith College.

1964   Spring: undergoes abdominal operation, in the aftermath of which her lupus flares up.

1964   3 August: Flannery O'Connor dies in Milledgeville hospital.

1965   *Everything That Rises Must Converge* published.

1969   *Mystery and Manners*, an edited selection of occasional prose drawn from her lectures and essays, published.

1971   *Collected Stories* published: this volume contains all of the stories in her two previous collections; the early stories submitted in fulfillment of the requirements of her MFA degree; early versions of both novels, parts of which were originally published in story form; a brief segment of an uncompleted novel; and a late uncollected story.

1972   *Collected Stories* awarded National Book Award.

1

•••

Introduction

"She was a girl who started with a gift for cartooning and satire." So begins Robert Fitzgerald's excellent biographical and critical introduction to Flannery O'Connor's post-humous collection of stories, *Everything That Rises Must Converge.* As Fitzgerald goes on to explain, she went far beyond her beginnings, but elements of the cartoonist's techniques—caricature, emotional flatness, violence—are evident in her early stories and persist, in somewhat more subtle form, throughout her work. Like the caricaturist, who uses exaggeration and distortion in order to emphasize the character of his subject, O'Connor created bizarre characters or extreme situations in order to attain "deeper kinds of realism"[1] than the sociological realism that she felt the popular spirit of the mid-twentieth century demanded of the writer. She appealed to the example of Hawthorne and to the "modern romance tradition" in defense of the writer who believes, as she did, that "our life is and will remain essentially mysterious."[2]

A major premise of O'Connor's thinking is that the realm of the Holy interpenetrates this world and affects it. It is the workings of this mystery that she was most concerned with demonstrating in her fiction. By her own explanation, the grotesquerie of her stories is directly related to her Christian perspective. This is a point that has bothered some critics, who feel that a Christian view of life ought to tend

1

toward the reconciliation of opposites, toward wholeness and affirmation, whereas the grotesque is by definition distorted, incomplete, or incongruous. To these critics O'Connor might have responded that they were trying to claim what has not been fully achieved: while opposites might be reconciled in Christ, the world was not yet reconciled to Him; we may know of the existence of wholeness because of Christ, but we are not yet whole ourselves. O'Connor's Christian conception of wholeness gave her the background against which she saw man in his present condition as, at best, incomplete; even the good, she felt, has a grotesque face, because "in us the good is something under construction."[3]

O'Connor found elements of her Christian vision of man in both the religion and history of her native region. The legacy of a revivalistic past has lingered longer in the South than in any other region of the country, and while O'Connor hesitated to describe the South as Christ-centered, she did feel it to be Christ-haunted. The South's history included a major experience—the loss of the Civil War—in which O'Connor found important theological implications. She saw the loss of the Civil War as the South's collective and personal experience of the biblical story of the Fall.

O'Connor relates that when novelist Walker Percy was asked why the South had so many good writers, he replied, "Because we lost the War." Commenting on his remark, O'Connor observed that Percy

didn't mean by that simply that a lost war makes good subject matter. What he was saying was that we have had our Fall. We have gone into the modern world with an inburnt knowledge of human limitations and with a sense of mystery which could not have developed in our first state of innocence—as it has not sufficiently developed in the rest of our country.[4]

Certainly not all Southerners—not even O'Connor's characters—have anything like "an inburnt knowledge of human limitations." Most of her characters, in fact, suffer from a refusal of such knowledge, and the thrust of most of her stories is to bring them to experience it. But she felt that on some level a biblical understanding of the human condition continued to operate in the South, and that its presence was reflected, even if it was largely unarticulated as such, in Southern literature.

Whenever I'm asked why Southern writers particularly have a penchant for writing about freaks, I say it is because we are still able to recognize one. To be able to recognize a freak, you have to have some conception of the whole man, and in the South the general conception of man is still, in the main, theological.[5]

Here again she emphasizes the connection between grotesquerie—"writing about freaks"—and theological vision, and touches on the deeper implications of the grotesque in literature.

Originally a term used to describe a mixture of styles in painting, "grotesque" has come to be used in literature to refer to characters who are physically or psychically abnormal, and to bizarre and extreme situations, especially those in which contradictory elements, such as comedy and horror, are mixed. An essential quality of the grotesque is incongruity, the mixture of things that do not normally occur—or seem to belong—together. In American literature, the grotesque is an offshoot of the fictional form that Hawthorne designated as "romance" to distinguish it from the traditional novel.

Henry James defined the essence of romance as "the disconnected and uncontrolled experience . . . uncontrolled by our general sense of 'the way things happen.'"[6] The extremes and contradictions characteristic of romance seem to be an expression of the conditions that shaped the American experience—the Puritan heritage, the existence of the wilderness and the frontier, the fact of slavery. The American imagination, as reflected in the work of our greatest

writers—Hawthorne, Melville, Twain, Faulkner—has been
(as Richard Chase has observed) more at home among the
extremes of experience, or in the violence and grotesquerie
of frontier humor, than in the more domestic social land-
scape of the novel as it flourished in England.

The techniques of romance can, of course, be exploited
for atmosphere and sensationalism, and can be used to
sentimentalize reality rather than plumb its deeper levels.
This is what has tended to happen in the Southern Gothic
novel. But in the hands of the masters of American fiction,
romance has proved to be a powerful medium for the ex-
ploration of fundamental problems that myth, literature, and
religion have raised since their earliest beginnings—problems
of sin and guilt, of good and evil. The pervasive sense of
contradiction that Richard Chase finds characteristic of our
best novels raises existential questions relating not only to
man's place in society but to his sense of his place in the
universe.

In literature that is usually described as grotesque, the
techniques of romance—exaggeration, distortion, violence,
the use of extreme situations—have been intensified. Accordingly, the questions about the meaning of life raised by
the grotesque tend to be even more insistent than those
raised by romance. The critic Gilbert Muller sees the incongruities of the grotesque as the expression of man's sense of
"the radical discontinuity of things," his awareness of "a
universe which is disjointed and senseless." In Muller's view,
the vision of grotesque literature "presents existence as de-
prived of meaning."[7] Given this interpretation, the logical
development of the grotesque vision is toward the literature
of the absurd.

O'Connor does use grotesque techniques to evoke a
world empty of meaning, which she saw as the condition of
the modern world cut off from its roots in the Holy, in
Being. The city of Taulkinham in *Wise Blood*, for instance,
is as grotesque and comically reduced a world as one will

find anywhere in modern literature. But she also used the same techniques of extremity, incongruity, and violence to break through the surface of her characters' (and, presumably, her readers') conceptions of reality and to penetrate into the hidden mystery of Being beneath. Finally, she used the grotesque as a way of expressing the incommensurability between the divine and the human, and in her work the violent techniques of the grotesque reflect the violence done to human sensibilities in the encounter with the Holy.

It goes without saying that O'Connor demands a great deal of the reader, not only in terms of his willingness to be open to her *données*, but also in terms of his willingness to let himself be illuminated by the light with which she searches her characters. But to read O'Connor well—to be aware of the depth of meaning of the stories as well as their surface humor, to perceive O'Connor's intelligence and understanding as well as her craftsmanship—is well worth the effort of receptiveness, and the repeated readings, and the reflection, which may be required.

Except in the case of a clearly autobiographical novelist, such as Thomas Wolfe or Henry Miller, it is difficult to assess the relationship between the circumstances of a writer's personal life and his fictional creation. The writer's raw materials are provided by his life experience, and he must write of what he knows, or can convincingly imagine, of the behavior of human beings in a particular place and time. To this elementary degree, the writer's life is inevitably related to his work. Beyond this, however, it is a tricky business to probe the writer's psyche to find the sources of his art. So much must remain unknown, so much more merely speculative. This is especially so in the case of O'Connor, whose life was short, and who gave the impression of being a very private person.

Born in Savannah in 1925, Mary Flannery O'Connor was the only child of Edwin Francis and Regina Cline

O'Connor. Both her parents came from Catholic families
that had lived for generations in the South. Her mother's
family had been prominent in Milledgeville, Georgia, and it
was to the white-pillared Cline house in the center of
Milledgeville that the O'Connors moved when Flannery's
father became ill with a fatal disease in the late 1930s.
Flannery had attended parochial schools in Savannah; in
Milledgeville she went to public high school and then to
Georgia State College for Women.

Ever since childhood she had had a fascination with
incongruities. In an essay on her hobby of raising peacocks
she tells of having, when she was five years old, a chicken
that could walk backward and forward. The chicken somehow attracted the attention of Pathé news, who sent a
cameraman to photograph it for a newsreel. This experience
so impressed her that "what had been only a mild interest
[chickens] became a passion, a quest. I had to have more
and more chickens. I favored those with one green eye and
one orange or with overlong necks and crooked combs. I
wanted one with three legs or three wings but nothing in that
line turned up."[8] Later, when her sewing class was instructed to make doll clothes, she made a "white piqué coat
with a lace collar and two buttons in the back" for a gray
bantam named Colonel Eggbert, and brought the chicken to
school to model his new outfit.

Were these the responses of an odd child who would
grow up to be, as Martha Stephens declares, a writer "pos-
sessed of so eccentric, at times so . . . repugnant a view of
human life that the strain of trying to enter emotionally into
her work is often very great indeed"?[9] Does her penchant
for odd fowl reflect some inarticulate awareness that she
herself was an "odd bird"? Or does it reflect something less
personal, something having to do with what she felt was "the
mystery of our position on earth"?[10]

Certainly her fascination with incongruity ran deep; it
is present in all of her writings both stylistically and themat-

ically. Incongruity embodied for her a fundamental human reality: man's experience of himself as a creature of both flesh and spirit, a being that is rooted in nature but that longs to transcend nature. Most of O'Connor's characters find this position intolerable and attempt to escape from it in a variety of ways; Mr. Shiftlet, in "The Life You Save May Be Your Own," identifies the body with a house and the spirit with an automobile and opts for fleeing with the automobile, implicitly refusing the pain and contradictions of existence in an earthbound body. Mrs. May in "Greenleaf" —like the numerous other hard-working, practical farm managers in O'Connor's stories—thinks fatuously that her control of her farm extends to the control of life: "I'll die when I get good and ready!" Only the old prophet Mason Tarwater (to my mind her most successful and most positive character) embraces with gusto the contradictory givens of the human condition—the fact of being a creature of both body and spirit, the fact that to fully embrace life one must also embrace death. And it is surely O'Connor's judgement on the perception of the rest of the world that old Tarwater is considered by most of the characters in the book—and also by some critics—to be crazy.

"I'm a born Catholic," O'Connor said in an interview near the end of her life, "and death has always been brother to my imagination."[11] More than most Catholics, however, she was faced early with the necessity of preparing for death, and this fact is surely related to the importance that death assumes in her fiction. Late in 1950, when she was twenty-five years old, she became seriously ill with disseminated lupus, the disease from which her father had died nine years before. Lupus causes the body to produce antibodies that attack its own tissues, and affects the blood, joints, and internal organs. By 1950, the use of cortisone made its prognosis somewhat brighter, but there is still no known cure.

When her illness struck, Flannery O'Connor had been

away from home for five years. After graduation from Georgia State College for Women in 1945, she had gone to the University of Iowa, where she received a Master of Fine Arts Degree in creative writing in 1947. Following a year at the Yaddo Writers' colony at Saratoga Springs, New York, she lived for a few months in New York City and then became a boarder with the family of the poet Robert Fitzgerald in Connecticut. By 1950 she had published six stories and was hard at work on a novel, begun three years earlier, for which she had already won a prize for a novel-in-progress. En route to Milledgeville for Christmas that year she became seriously ill and had to be hospitalized in Atlanta.

Though Catholicism's view of death as an infinite widening of life's circle, not as its closing, may have been fully acceptable to her intellectually, one can hardly assume that coming to grips with it existentially was for O'Connor an easy matter. For one thing, she must have suffered a great deal from the physical discomfort of the illness itself, to which was added the discomfort of the side effects of the cortisone used to treat it. Even more important was the suffering she must have experienced in being forced out beyond the borders of safety, out into the darkness of the unknown and the uncontrollable where death may be waiting, where one's life is no longer in one's own hands, but in the hands of God. Given her faith, O'Connor must have considered it her task to bring herself to full consent to the fact of her own powerlessness, to put herself unconditionally at the disposal of God. It is not hard to see some connection between this and the terrifying aspect the transcendent often assumes in her stories.

Certainly the stories she wrote after the onset of her illness were different from those[12] that preceded it, both in sheer power and in the insistent presence in them of questions about the meaning of life and death, questions raised in such a way as to preclude easy answers. Her illness did not, of course, change her fundamental view of life, but it brought home to her the *experience* of human limitation, which, she later said, she believed to be the "bedrock of all human experience" and the experience in which the fiction writer is most interested. Though she was concerned with essential, rather than simply physical, limitation, she saw the latter as the symbol of the former. The actual poor, she felt, "live with less padding between them and the raw forces of life," but for the writer the poor symbolize "the state of all men."[13] Similarly, I think she saw the physical limitations placed on her life after her illness as a symbolic expression of that essential human limitation, the limitation of finitude.

In any event, she was confined to what many would consider a narrow existence. If, as the five years spent away from home suggest, she had intended to create a life for herself away from the South, that was no longer possible. When she was released from the hospital, she and her mother moved to a dairy farm outside Milledgeville that her mother had recently inherited and was running with the help of tenants. O'Connor was still being treated with large doses of cortisone, which made her face puffy and her hair fall out, and for some time she was on a special diet. Yet a phenomenal creative energy was at work. She finished her first novel, *Wise Blood* (1952), a strange, original, fierce book, and she began to write stories—"A Good Man Is Hard to Find," "The Life You Save May Be Your Own"— that in their way, as Robert Fitzgerald observes, are as good as anything she ever did. She worked for three hours in the morning, relaxed in the afternoon, and indulged her fondness for fowl by acquiring a variety of ducks, geese, chickens, and finally peacocks. Within a few years her disease, or the drugs used to combat it, or both, caused a deterioration of the bones in her hips so that she was obliged to use a cane and, finally, crutches.

Nevertheless, she seems to have felt her limitations to be a source of strength. Fitzgerald reports that, sent on a trip to Lourdes by "Cousin Katie in Savannah," O'Connor "dreaded the possibility of a miracle," and "forced herself to the piety of the bath for her mother's sake and Cousin Katie's."[14] This seems to be a puzzling attitude for her to have taken, unless she considered her illness, and the resultant day-to-day confrontation with her own mortality, the means whereby she was coming to know herself, both as a Christian and as a writer. Her way of encountering mortality was not simply to learn to accept it—which implies a rather supine and long-suffering endurance of what cannot be changed—but, like old Tarwater, to meet it with a certain gusto. This is not to suggest that she found her situation easy, or that there was not some mockery of herself (or the person she might have been) in all those stories of grown children living, more or less embattled, with their mothers on Southern dairy farms. The particular life she was given to live was a hard one, but she met its challenge and, in so doing, was brought beyond herself—beyond the person she might have been had her life been more normal.

Richard Gilman suggests that this is the case in his description of his meeting with O'Connor in 1960. Uncertain and afraid of his response to the ravages of her illness, he found himself at first averting his eyes:

But then, as we talked, something broke and I was looking at her, at her face twisted to one side, at her stiff and somewhat puffy hands and arms, and at her thinning and lusterless hair. From then on, although I would be shaken by an occasional spasm of pity I hated feeling, her appearance was absorbed for me into her presence and—I don't use the word lightly—transfigured by it.

Tough-minded, laconic, with a marvelous wit and an absolute absence of self-pity, she made me understand, as never before or since, what spiritual heroism and beauty can be. There was nothing soft in it, no "radiance," no conventional serenity. She could exhibit impatience, doubt, pleasure in compliments, great distress at unfavorable reviews. But she was almost entirely free from calculation, from any concern with what might be expected of her, and from any desire to question her fate or move into outrage.[15]

During the last half-dozen years of life O'Connor enjoyed a growing recognition of her work. Her first collection of short stories, *A Good Man Is Hard to Find*, appeared in 1955, and her second novel, *The Violent Bear It Away*, in 1960. At the time few reviewers saw beneath the grotesque surface of her fiction (Granville Hicks called *The Violent Bear It Away* "Southern Gothic with a vengeance") but she was almost unanimously regarded as a writer of originality and power. What was to become a substantial body of criticism of her work began to grow in the wake of her essay "The Fiction Writer and His Country" (1957), in which she discussed the apparent contradiction between her belief in spiritual purpose and the fact that her stories are, "for the most part, about people who are poor, who are afflicted in both mind and body, who have little—or at best distorted— sense of spiritual purpose, and whose actions do not apparently give the reader a great assurance of the joy of life."[16] She also began to be invited to lecture at colleges and writers' conferences, where she spoke on such subjects as "Some Aspects of the Grotesque in Southern Fiction" and "The Catholic Novelist in the Protestant South." (The drafts of these speeches: plus some other essays, were collected and edited by Sally and Robert Fitzgerald under the title *Mystery and Manners*, 1969.)

O'Connor continued to refine the art in which she expressed her vision, but the vision itself did not substantially change from the stories in *A Good Man Is Hard to Find* to those in her final collection, *Everything That Rises Must Converge* (posthumously published 1965). She spoke once, near the end of her life, of attempting something different from what she had been doing so successfully, but in the final months of her life she was still at work on the stories that were to complete her last collection. Following an abdominal operation in the spring of 1964, her lupus flared up again. She survived its onslaught for a few months, but late in July she suffered kidney failure. She died on August 3, 1964, at the age of 39.

2

•••

A Good Man Is Hard to Find

In most of the stories in *A Good Man Is Hard to Find* there is a considerable difference between the subjective point of view of the protagonist and the objective point of view supplied by the author. O'Connor mingles the two points of view with extreme skill, one shading into the other from sentence to sentence, so that both are maintained almost simultaneously. This double point of view is one of the many forms of irony that characterize O'Connor's work. Most simply, irony results when the tone of what is said indicates that another (and usually opposite) meaning is intended than the meaning conveyed by the face value of the words. In O'Connor's stories there is typically a strong tension between literal meaning and tone, or between the character's evaluation of himself and his situation and the actuality of the situation that the omniscient author suggests through carefully controlled tone and imagery.

The style of most of the stories is deliberately kept flat,[1] and their ironic, often unsettling conclusions seem to mock or deny both conventional expectations and commonly accepted human values. Beneath the grotesquerie of the surface, however, a deeper level of meaning is suggested by tonal shifts and by various significant cues and allusions. For instance, religious allusions and conventional platitudes are present in most of the stories as part of the cultural baggage of the characters, and are apparently not to be taken seriously. The evident meaninglessness of these allusions constitutes one level of irony. O'Connor creates another level of irony by using these very platitudes for their literal meaning, as signs pointing to the mystery that the action of the story as a whole is intended to evoke.

The transcendent (by which I mean all that which is more than human) is introduced through symbols, through symbolic action, or simply through a character's persistent (and often negative) concern with it. However, O'Connor's images of the transcendent often include something contradictory to our usual sense of what the transcendent is. When O'Connor employs the sun, or a thundercloud, as a symbol, she does so mindful of their long history as symbols of divine power; but she frequently adds some discordant element to enforce her point that her characters fundamentally sense divine power as a threat to their image of what they are—this despite their frequent appeals to God or their belief that they are on His side. Thus the sentimentalizing con man Mr. Shiftlet, after calling on God to "break forth and wash the slime from this earth," is himself pursued by a comic-grotesque image of God in the form of a turnip-shaped thundercloud emitting a "guffawing peal of thunder."

Similarly, when O'Connor creates an image pointing to the action of the transcendent in the world, that image is likely to be what her characters and readers alike experience as grotesque (the freak in "A Temple of the Holy Ghost"), profoundly ambiguous (the Negroes, real and artificial, in "The Artificial Nigger"), or ludicrous (the theft of Hulga's wooden leg in "Good Country People"). The agents through which the transcendent operates are not likely to appear beneficent; the three mean poor-white boys in "A Circle in the Fire" are compared to the young prophets dancing in the fiery furnace to reinforce O'Connor's perception of them as agents of transcendent power, but their intent as individuals in setting fire to Mrs. Cope's woods is simply malicious. An action in which O'Connor sees transcendent meaning often has results that, seen from an anthropocentric point of view, are horrifying. The scene at the end of "A Good Man Is Hard to Find" is littered with dead bodies. The little boy Harry Ashfield of "The River" drowns himself trying to make his baptism into "the Kingdom of Christ" a literal reality.

The ironies and contradictions expressed in O'Connor's handling of the transcendent are all an intrinsic part of the point she wished to convey: that from the anthropocentric point of view of her characters, the divine is felt as an intrusion, an affront, a destructive force. It "upset[s] the balance" (as Mrs. McIntyre says of the Christ-like Mr. Guizac in "The Displaced Person"); it upsets the balance of the human world, it breaks and shatters.

O'Connor made this point so forcefully that one critic has charged her religious view with being "forbidding" and "oppressive."[2] Loss, suffering, and death can be regarded only as evils for the humanist who sees good and evil largely in terms of material well-being. In O'Connor's stories, however, suffering and death are often the means through which a character is brought from what O'Connor regarded as a superficial or narrow understanding of life to some experience of the mystery in which, she believed, we live and move and have our being.

O'Connor typically uses techniques that inflict shock and violence upon the reader as the means of making the level of manners (the surface action) transparent to the level of mystery. In addition to his vicarious experience of the violence suffered by the characters, the reader is subjected to a violence done to his expectations in the ironic and often horrific twists that end many O'Connor tales.

Though violence, suffering and death are ubiquitous elements in O'Connor's work, her stories are nevertheless unquestionably comic. One of her primary themes—incongruity—is in itself the very stuff of comedy. All comedy

grows out of the humorous effect of incongruity; it depends
on a gap—and a somehow ironic or fitting one—between
what is expected and what actually happens. Incongruity is
not easily borne when we ourselves are the subject of it, but
given the proper setting and a mood of detachment, we can
laugh for hours about incongruous situations in the lives of
others. There is evidently a certain release of tension to be
found in laughing at situations that could, if they were presented seriously, be experienced as painful or even tragic.

It seems to me that a major root of comedy is in our
fear of losing human dignity, coupled with our apprehension
that there is nothing in the nature of the universe to support
human dignity; it is a very precarious commodity—as precarious as the balance of a man slipping on a banana peel.
When the tension of that fear can be released in safe situations—for instance, through the highly conventional form of
traditional comedy—we can experience a great sense of enjoyment, relief, and a temporary freedom from an omnipres-
ent anxiety.

In classical comedy, the incongruities of the action
could be safely enjoyed because the traditional comic form
ended in reconciliation; whatever was amiss and out of joint
at the beginning would be set right at the end. Chaos was
exposed and enjoyed temporarily, but the primacy of order
and harmony was reaffirmed at the end. In modern comedy,
however—I am thinking especially of the work of Beckett,
Ionesco, and Pinter—this final affirmation of faith in the
basic order of the universe is lacking. This type of modern
comedy ends not in the classical reconciliation scene but in a
parody of it. It compounds the incongruities and dislocations
out of which comedy is made by insisting on final incongruities, and in so doing it evokes both laughter and horror.

Like Pinter and Ionesco, O'Connor mixes comedy and
horror. However, there is an important difference between
the ends to which she and these modern playwrights put
their comic techniques. Pinter and Ionesco exploit clichés

and banal language in order to finally transform language, which we take for granted as something fundamentally orderly and meaningful, into a medium for directly evoking disorder and meaninglessness. The initial effect of two couples assaulting each other with platitudes in Ionesco's play *The Bald Soprano* is funny; but the breakdown of meaning that the language progressively suffers becomes increasingly menacing.

Instead of breaking down language to demonstrate a fundamental meaninglessness, O'Connor uses mixed comedy and horror to break down her characters' (and also her readers') conventional way of looking at the world; but once the conventional vision has been thoroughly destroyed, she usually suggests that the experience of shock, horror, or death has stripped her characters of their pretensions and brought them into contact with a fundamental order grounded in divine mystery.

"A Good Man Is Hard to Find" demonstrates O'Connor's technique of revealing the hollowness of the protagonist's conventional understanding of order, of destroying the conventional order, and finally of suggesting the existence of a profound but appallingly demanding order beneath it. She begins by establishing the gap between the order believed in by the protagonist, a comically genteel grandmother, and the lack of order revealed in the actual situation. Setting out with her family on their vacation trip to Florida, the grandmother responds to the undisciplined behavior of her grandchildren with the observation that in her time "children were more respectful. . . . People did right then." Seeing a naked Negro child in the door of a roadside shack, she exclaims, "Oh look at the cute little pickanniny!", oblivious to the realities of poverty and racism the scene implies.

At the same time, O'Connor uses the literal meaning of the grandmother's words to indicate the main themes of the story. When the family stops for lunch at a roadside restaurant, the grandmother has a comically platitudinous exchange with the proprietor, Red Sammy Butts:

"A good man is hard to find," Red Sammy said. "Everything is getting terrible. I remember the day you could go off and leave your screen door unlatched. Not no more."

He and the grandmother discussed better times. The old lady said that in her opinion Europe was entirely to blame for the way things were now. She said the way Europe acted you would think we were made of money and Red Sam said it was no use talking about it, she was exactly right.

These words, empty as they are in the mouths of these characters, underscore the main themes of the story: the fact that the world is, indeed, out of joint, and the question of what constitutes a good man (or a good woman).

The action of the story brings the grandmother from an understanding of goodness in conventional terms (being a lady) to a glimpse of O'Connor's theological understanding of goodness. This is brought about by the grandmother's encounter with The Misfit, an escaped killer who comes upon the family when their car overturns on an isolated road. While his companions lead the rest of the family off into the woods to be shot, The Misfit, a thoughtful, scholarly-looking man in steel-rimmed spectacles, engages the grandmother in conversation. His experience of life has convinced him that things do not add up, that justice does not exist: "I can't make what all I done wrong fit what all I gone through in punishment." He has come to the conclusion that there are no sure foundations on which order and meaning can be built, and that, in the absence of meaning, there is "no pleasure in life but meanness."

In terms of the world evoked in the story, The Misfit's perception of a fundamental lack of order and justice in the universe is more in accord with what actually is than is the grandmother's belief in the ordering power of conventional decorum and conventional religion. The actuality of alienation and disorder is suggested in the first half of the story through the petty wrangling within the grandmother's family and through the underlying sense of sterility that pervades the atmosphere. However, despite the grandmother's complaint that "People are certainly not nice like they used to be," her perception of the disorder of the world is as superficial as her understanding of good. The grandmother does not *experience* the actuality of disorder until her encounter with The Misfit.

Richard Pearce, in his analysis of modern comedy called *Stages of the Clown* (1970), has made some perceptive observations on O'Connor's work. He finds that she uses the clown—i.e., the grotesque figure, the freak, the madman, the outsider—"to turn the world upside down," to startle both protagonist and reader into "fresh views of contemporary reality."[3] The Misfit clearly does that; he demolishes conventional order, and the terror he creates is all the more chilling because he retains the forms of polite behavior in the midst of the most inhuman acts. His actions demonstrate a complete lack of essential connection between conventional behavior and some fundamental standard of good and evil that is assumed to lie behind it. He apologizes for not wearing a shirt in the presence of ladies, and he asks the children's mother to accompany his companions into the woods—to be shot—with the utmost politeness. Because of the extreme incongruity between his demeanor and his actions, his actions are not only felt as an intrusion of violence, which temporarily destroys order, but as an intrusion of meaninglessness, which questions the existence of any foundations on which order can be built.

However, as Pearce goes on to point out, having turned the conventional world upside down and revealed the existence of a world in which order and justice do not obtain, O'Connor characteristically brings about a "second inversion" through which "she rediscovers essential truths, transvalues values, and affirms a primal order." For the reader not intuitively in accord with her view of life, the question may be whether she accomplishes this second inversion as effectively as the first. There is no doubt, however, that she intends to affirm order, and to do it in such a way that both protagonist and reader are potentially brought to see that there is a deep meaning behind conventional expressions of order that they had previously been unaware of.

It was O'Connor's conviction that this moment of insight (or moment of grace, as she sometimes called it) was not come by easily. Frequently it comes to her characters at the moment of their own death. In "A Good Man Is Hard to Find" this moment comes when the conventional order to which the grandmother has all her life given lip service has been thoroughly broken down by the terror of the experience she is undergoing. She has seen her family taken away into the woods, she has heard the shots, and she has desperately kept up a conversation with The Misfit, urging him to pray in the futile hope that if he acknowledged conventional religion he would not shoot her. Her appeals to Jesus have prompted The Misfit to reflect on the implications of Jesus's existence:

"If He did what He said, then it's nothing for you to do but throw away everything and follow Him, and if He didn't, then it's nothing for you to do but enjoy the few minutes you got left the best way you can—by killing somebody or burning down his house or doing some other meanness to him."

The grandmother's response—"Maybe He didn't raise the dead"—suggests that her conventional religious faith is breaking down; it may be dawning on her that the very existence of The Misfit posits a possibility that had never occurred to her before, that perhaps there *is* no order and meaning in life, that perhaps Jesus did not do what He said. O'Connor adds that the old lady did not know what she was saying, thus emphasizing the extreme confusion that the grandmother experiences when her superficial pattern of seeing and responding is broken. But this breakdown makes possible the emergence of a new perception, which occurs when The Misfit displays the urgency of his concern over whether or not Jesus raised the dead:

"I wasn't there so I can't say He didn't [raise the dead]," The Misfit said. "I wisht I had of been there," he said, hitting the ground with his fist. "It ain't right I wasn't there because if I had of been there I would of known. Listen lady," he said in a high voice, "if I had of been there I would of known and I wouldn't be like I am now."

When the old lady hears his words, spoken in a voice that seems "about to crack," O'Connor tells us that "the grandmother's head cleared for an instant." She sees The Misfit (who is now wearing her murdered son's shirt) as one of her own children, and she reaches out to touch him.

What is the meaning of this gesture? O'Connor thought it was critically important, and she used it as an example of "what makes a story work":

I have decided that it [what makes a story work] is probably some action, some gesture of a character that is unlike any other in the story, one which indicates where the real heart of the story lies. This would have to be an action or a gesture which was both totally right and totally unexpected; it would have to be one that was both in character and beyond character; it would have to suggest both the world and eternity.[4]

The grandmother's words—"Why you're one of my babies. You're one of my own children!"—and her gesture of reaching out to The Misfit indicate that Pearce's "second inversion" has taken place. Out of the chaos following the breakdown of her conventional belief in order, she comes to a recognition that is actual and not simply platitudinous of the mystery of human connectedness. As O'Connor explained to an audience to whom she was reading this story, the grandmother realizes, "even in her limited way, that she is responsible for the man before her and joined to him by ties of kinship which have their roots deep in the mystery she has been merely prattling about so far."[5]

The Misfit's response to the grandmother's gesture is unexpected and violent. He springs back "as if a snake had bitten him" and shoots her three times through the chest. This shocking act is, I think, intended to accomplish the "second inversion" in the reader, to make him feel the significance of the grandmother's gesture in the violence of The Misfit's response to it. Whether or not the reader consciously works out its implications, if he perceives the grandmother's gesture as having some kind of depth and clarity, in contrast to the comic flatness of her earlier actions, he is in touch with the heart of the story.

The concluding lines of the story recall the theme suggested by the title, the scarcity of good men. Having killed the grandmother, The Misfit observes, "She would of been a good woman . . . if it had been somebody there to shoot her every minute of her life." The price of being a "good woman" is living with an awareness of death. O'Connor suggests that to be truly human—to be a "good man"—is to accept one's mortality and one's solidarity with all human suffering. As the title and most of the stories in the collection suggest, O'Connor was of the opinion that a good man is hard to find.

In both "A Stroke of Good Fortune" and "A Late Encounter with the Enemy," the "enemy," from the protagonists' point of view, is time, history, and mortality. Ruby Hill, the protagonist of the earlier story, is obsessed with keeping her youth. Having seen her mother become an old woman at thirty-four through frequent pregnancies, Ruby is determined to avoid growing old by avoiding childbearing. The irony of her attempt to avoid death by, in effect, avoiding life is heavily stressed. Her inevitable mortality is emphasized by the description of her body: it is shaped "like a funeral urn." Her desperate attempts to deny this reality are reflected in her assertions about herself: she thinks of herself as "extremely young looking for her age," and reflects with pride that "somebody as alive as her" had come out of her "dried-up" family. The story turns on her growing realization that, in spite of precautions, she is pregnant. The growth of life in her she regards as something "to make her deader," and she is left at the end of the story contemplating it with horror.

"A Late Encounter with the Enemy" is, in externals, a satire on the Southern cult of the past. Sally Poker Sash, a sixty-two-year-old schoolteacher, has been resentfully going to summer school for the past twenty years to get her degree. She intends to have her grandfather, a one-hundred-four-year-old Civil War veteran, on the stage at her graduation as a symbol of "what all was behind her":

Glorious upright old man standing for the old traditions! Dignity! Honor! Courage!

However, the old man is an empty relic exploited as a symbol of something he is not. Though known as General Tennessee Flintrock Sash, his real name is George Poker Sash. He was probably only a foot soldier, and he has no memory of the war at all. He has no use for the painful realities of history; only one event in his past has any significance to him, and that is the role he played at the premiere of the movie *Gone With the Wind*. At that event he was given a general's uniform and seated on the stage with the celebrities. O'Connor's implied judgement on the romanticization of the past, and the refusal to confront the realities of time, history, and mortality, is obvious.

The story concludes with the general's forced encounter with history in the moments preceding his death. While the graduation procession wends its way toward the auditorium, the general is left hatless in his wheelchair in the blazing August sun. (O'Connor characteristically uses the sun as a symbol of transcendent power.) The general feels as if the sun were burning a little hole in the top of his head. When he is brought inside the auditorium and seated on the stage, the procession of black-gowned graduates marching toward him seems to him to be the "black procession" of history. He tries to resist his growing awareness of the tide of history, but the words of the history-invoking commencement speaker "kept seeping in through the little hole in his head." The words come at him "like musket fire," and as his forgotten history comes back to him, "he felt his body riddled in a hundred places with sharp stabs of pain." At the moment of his death, in a desperate effort to grasp the meaning of history, "to find out what comes after the past," he clenches his hand on his bare sword "until the blade touched bone."

There is an implied comparison between the complexities and ambiguities of the general's remembered past—"his wife's narrow face looking at him critically ... one of his squinting bald-headed sons ... his mother ... [running] toward him with an anxious look"—and the romanticized past that he symbolizes for Sally Poker Sash, who holds her head "a perceptible degree higher" as she crosses the stage in front of the dead and staring general to receive her degree. The story ends with an image suggesting the triviality of the present in which the past is so falsified. After the graduation ceremony is over, Sally Poker's Boy Scout nephew, in charge of wheeling the general about, bumps him "at high speed down a flagstone path" and waits, "with the corpse, in the long line at the Coca-Cola machine."

In neither of these stories is there much sense that the protagonist understands or accepts the realities of human existence that are being thrust upon him. Similarly, in "The Life You Save May Be Your Own," the revelation is to the reader more than to the protagonist, Mr. Shiftlet. A one-armed drifter with a passion for automobiles, Mr. Shiftlet is a man always on the move. Fast-talking and sly, he acquires an automobile by marrying the owner's deaf-and-dumb daughter Lucynell, and then rids himself of the unwanted girl by leaving her at a roadside restaurant a hundred miles from home. The comic tone of the story leads the reader to expect Mr. Shiftlet to have a change of heart and go back and get Lucynell. (In fact, when the story was adapted for a television production some years ago, a conventional happy ending was substituted for O'Connor's more difficult and demanding one.) In so frustrating the reader's expectations, O'Connor intended to move the story out of the realm of simple backwoods comedy and into the dimension of mystery.

The dimension of mystery is introduced into the story initially in an ironic way through Mr. Shiftlet's sentimental statements about the mystery of the human heart, about responsibility for others, about man being a creature of body and spirit. In Mr. Shiftlet's mouth these statements contribute to the comedy of the story because they are so patently a part of the trickster's spiel. If O'Connor had given her story the conventionally expected ending, there would be no reason to examine these statements more closely. As it is, however, in breaking the comic literary convention, she forces the reader to look at the whole story in a different light, and to question the implications of Mr. Shiftlet's words and actions.

Mr. Shiftlet then becomes a figure of modern man—man always on the move but with a destinationless motion. (The pun on his intended destination at the end of the story—Mobile—is too obvious not to be significant.) His identification of the body with a house, rooted in the earth, and the spirit with an automobile, always on the move, reflects O'Connor's conviction that her age suffered from a Manichaean sensibility that considers the body and the spirit to be incompatible and that tends to seek transcendence, or freedom, through an escape from the limitations and absurdities of the flesh.

Much of O'Connor's fiction seems deliberately intended to affront this Manichaean sensibility by depicting the flesh in its more grotesque and repulsive forms and at the same time insisting that it is *this* flesh, not something etherealized and beautiful, in which the spirit dwells. She seems to have written out of a curious kind of love for material creation— curious, because it does not express itself in the usual way, as a straightforward celebration of natural beauty. But it is love nevertheless, because of her insistence that the lowest and ugliest and most grotesque of creatures are no less capable than the intelligent and well-formed of being indwelt by the spirit. Moreover, she insisted that transcendence is to be found not through escaping from the limitations of the body but, paradoxically, through embracing physical realities that the human mind tends to find repellent.

This paradox is at the heart of her fiction, and it is perhaps significant that the story in which she deals with it most explicitly—"A Temple of the Holy Ghost"—is located in the center of this collection. "A Temple of the Holy Ghost" is atypical both in its lack of a sudden turnabout at the end and in its use of specifically Catholic imagery. It reflects what O'Connor referred to as "the Catholic sacramental view of life," the belief that, appearances notwithstanding, the transcendent operates in and through the natural world. The story deals with the experience of a twelve-year-old Catholic child who, though bratty and far from pious, has a genuine religious sensibility that breaks through from time to time.

Through her boy-crazy second cousins, who come for a weekend visit from their convent school, the child is exposed to images that strongly take hold of her imagination. The girls have just been told by Sister Perpetua, the oldest nun in their school, that if a boy should " 'behave in an ungentlemanly manner with them in the back seat of an automobile,' " they were to say " 'Stop sir! I am a Temple of the Holy Ghost!' " They find this idea so ludicrous that they are convulsed with laughter whenever they think of it. Hearing them tell about it, the child is struck by the image. "I am a Temple of the Holy Ghost, she said to herself, and was pleased with the phrase. It made her feel as if somebody had given her a present."

That evening the older girls see a hermaphrodite on display in a sideshow when their dates take them to the fair. The freak declares its acceptance of its grotesque condition: "God made me thisaway.... I don't dispute it." After her cousins tell her what they have seen, the child, in falling asleep, combines the mystery of the hermaphrodite (how could a person be a man and a woman both without having two heads, she wonders) with the talk about the Holy Ghost she heard earlier in the day. In her fantasy reconstruction of the scene, she imagines the men and women in the tent looking "more solemn than they were in church," and responding to the freak's words by saying "Amen. Amen."

> "God done this to me and I praise Him."
> "Amen. Amen." . . .
> ". . . You are God's temple, don't you know? . . . God's Spirit has a dwelling in you, don't you know?"
> "Amen. Amen."
> ". . . A temple of God is a holy thing. Amen. Amen."
> "I am a temple of the Holy Ghost."
> "Amen."

The next afternoon the child and her mother take the girls back to their convent school, and then attend the Sunday evening Benediction of the Blessed Sacrament. The Blessed Sacrament is the Body of Christ, sacramentally present in the consecrated Host, a round white wafer about three inches in diameter. In the service of Benediction the Host is exposed in a monstrance for the adoration of the faithful. While she is looking at the monstrance the child again thinks of the freak, and hears him say, "I don't dispute it. This is the way He wanted me to be."

In juxtaposing the grotesque condition of the freak with the sacramental image of Christ, O'Connor is emphasizing the grotesqueness—from the naturalistic point of view—of the union of the human and the divine in the person of

Jesus, just as she had emphasized the grotesqueness of the idea of the body being a temple of the Holy Spirit by associating that image with the freak. In so stressing the grotesqueness of these unions, she was trying to bring to the surface what she felt to be the deep and largely unconscious response of most of her audience—which is that the union of the grossly physical and the spiritual is grotesque. She would go so far, I think, as to say that this is a natural human response; we want to transcend our limitations by moving away from them, and any concept of transcendence that brings us back to physicality and suffering we are apt to reject.

Such a vision of the sacramental presence of Christ in the world as O'Connor offers in this story seems, indeed, grotesque. But she is not mocking the idea that the body is a temple of the Holy Ghost by holding up against it the image of fat, smelly, pig-eared Alonzo Myers, who drives the child and her mother home at the end of the story. Nor is she mocking the hermaphrodite's acceptance of the will of God because that Christ-like acceptance does not lighten the freak's humiliation or change its condition. In the face of these realities she upholds very seriously her belief that the freak, and Alonzo Myers, *are* temples of the Holy Ghost, and that, despite the suffering and ugliness of the world, Christ *is* sacramentally present in it. He is present not only as the transfigured and transcendent Christ suggested in the image of the "ivory sun," so bright the child could only look at it through the veil of her hair; he is also present as the suffering Christ suggested in the closing line of the story, in which the setting sun is compared to a Host dipped in blood. Indeed, O'Connor emphasizes the continuing, if hidden, presence of the suffering Christ on earth in the final image: the sun sets, but it leaves behind it a line in the sky "like a red clay road hanging over the trees."

O'Connor believed that Christ, by His incarnation and His continuing sacramental presence, entered into the suffering of the world in order to bring about its redemption, and that man is asked to accept and participate in that suffering. Most of her characters, however, are resolutely set on avoiding it. Mrs. Cope, of "A Circle in the Fire," is engaged in building impregnable defenses against suffering, defenses symbolized by the "fortress wall of trees" that surrounds her farm. The inadequacy of these defenses against the ubiquitous reality of human misery is suggested through Mrs. Cope's constant anxiety, and through the comic-grotesque tales of disaster constantly being retailed by her tenant's wife, Mrs. Pritchard. The uncontrollable disaster Mrs. Cope fears arrives in the form of three mean poor-white boys from the city who come initially to enjoy the pleasures of the country. Their annoyance with her possessive concern for her farm and "her" woods—"Gawd owns them woods and her too," one of them observes dryly—leads them to set her woods on fire. This destruction of her symbolic defenses makes Mrs. Cope vulnerable, at last, to suffering, and unites her with the suffering of the world. On her face, as she stares at the fire, is a look of "misery," a misery that "might have belonged to anybody, a Negro or a European [i.e., a displaced person] or to Powell [one of the poor-white boys] himself."

Despite the agony involved in it, O'Connor saw this experience of "misery" as something at least potentially able to heal the strivings for dominance and individual security that set men apart from one another. In "The Artificial Nigger" the estrangement between old Mr. Head and his young grandson Nelson is healed by the sight of a chipped plaster statue of a Negro with a look of "wild misery" on its face. This strange figure is described as a "monument to another's victory." Possibly this phrase refers to the "victory" of the white man over the Negro, but O'Connor almost certainly also had in mind the paradoxical victory of Christ suffering on the cross.

The sight of this figure—which the old man and the

boy come upon at the end of a long and exhausting day in a strange city—breaks down the barriers of pride and unforgiveness between them and brings them "together in their common defeat." In this defeat they lose the separateness from one another and from the whole of humanity that had characterized them throughout the story. The impulse of each to set himself above others is suggested in their own relationship—each constantly, and comically, jockeys for a position of dominance—and in their attitude of contempt and fear toward Negroes, which, in the story, come to represent not only a subject race but the mysterious and threatening Other. The experience of defeat not only brings them to share in the common lot of humanity, but is the source of an "action of mercy" that consumes Mr. Head's pride and brings him to feel that "he was forgiven for sins from the beginning of time . . . and ready at that instant to enter Paradise."

The first half of "The Displaced Person" is thematically similar to "A Circle in the Fire" and "The Artificial Nigger." Mrs. Shortley, the protagonist, is a gargantuan, almost burlesque, figure who has an exaggerated sense of her sovereignty over "her" domain. This sovereignty is ironic; the image of the "white afternoon sun . . . creeping behind a ragged wall of cloud as if it pretended to be an intruder" is a cue to the reader to remember that, in O'Connor's way of thinking, God owns the world and Mrs. Shortley too. The irony is doubled in that Mrs. Shortley is not even the legal owner of the world she considers hers; it is Mrs. McIntyre's farm, and Mrs. Shortley and her husband are tenants.

When Mrs. McIntyre brings in a Polish family of displaced persons to work on the farm, Mrs. Shortley regards them as a threat to the way things are in her world. Her classification of foreigners as Other is so extreme that she regards the Poles as less than human; the first thing that strikes her as peculiar when she meets them is that "they looked like other people. Every time she had seen them in her imagination, the image she had got was of the three bears, walking single file, with wooden shoes on like Dutchmen and sailor hats and bright coats with a lot of buttons." Though her assessment of their lack of intelligence ("They can't talk.... You reckon they'll know what colors even is?") is so exaggerated as to be comic in its effect, it makes clear her unquestioned assumption that these Others have no more relationship to her than if they had come from outer space. Indeed, it is not long before Mrs. Shortley comes to the conclusion that they are agents of the devil.

However, the Pole, Mr. Guizac, is so honest and industrious that he puts the lazy Mr. Shortley and the thieving Negroes in a bad light, and Mrs. McIntyre begins to hint that she may have to fire some of her other help in order to pay Mr. Guizac more. Seeing her world thus threatened, Mrs. Shortley is determined to prevent the Poles from displacing the Negroes; but she is so sure of her own place in her world that it does not even occur to her that she and Mr. Shortley might be the ones to be displaced. When this happens—she overhears that Mrs. McIntyre is planning to fire the Shortleys—she is beside herself with outrage. She immediately packs her family's belongings into the car in order to be on the road before the next day dawns. Her outrage and agitation, however, bring on a stroke. In her paroxysm she clutches at everything within her reach: "Mr. Shortley's head, [her daughter] Sarah Mae's leg, the cat, a wad of white bedding, her own big moon-like knee." The tangle of limbs in the crowded car implicitly recalls the heap of tangled bodies Mrs. Shortley had once seen in a war newsreel: "dead naked people all in a heap, their arms and legs tangled together, a head thrust in here, a head there, a foot, a knee...." Thus her experience of being displaced from Mrs. McIntyre's farm brings her to a condition imagistically parallel to that of the most displaced Europeans; in suffering and death she is united with suffering humanity. Her death is a breakthrough from separateness and isolation to expansiveness and vision. O'Connor observes that, though the others in the car are not aware of it, Mrs. Shortley "had had a great experience." In being displaced, by death, from the world she thought belonged to her, she comes to see "for the first time the tremendous frontiers of her true country."

In its original form (published in the *Sewanee Review*) "The Displaced Person" ended at this point. For its inclusion in *A Good Man Is Hard to Find*, O'Connor added on virtually another complete story, in which Mrs. McIntyre is the protagonist.[6] Mrs. McIntyre is a practical woman who initially regards the displaced person as her "salvation" because his thrifty, hard-working ways are saving her money. When, however, he attempts to get his sixteen-year-old cousin out of the displaced-persons camp by arranging to marry her to one of the Negro hands, Mrs. McIntyre instantly reverses her opinion of him. "He's extra.... He doesn't fit in.... He's upset the balance around here," she complains to the priest who had arranged for the Polish family to come.

The "balance around here" is not the equilibrium of true justice but a utilitarian balance Mrs. McIntyre believes she has precariously maintained in her thirty-year struggle against the rapacity of "the world's overflow" who have passed through her employ as tenants. She sees this balance largely in economic terms and insists that, because she pays the bills, the continuing orderly existence of the farm is dependent on her. "I'm the one around here who holds all the strings together," she tells one of her Negro hands. "You're all dependent on me." When Mr. Guizac's desire to rescue his cousin from the camp comes in conflict with the conventional ordering of Negro-white relations on the farm, Mrs. McIntyre opts for the preservation of order and wants to get rid of him. She repeatedly disclaims any responsibility for the "world's overflow"—all the people, whether from Poland or Tennessee, who are in one way or another displaced.

Mrs. McIntyre is, however, curiously unwilling to take

direct action against what is "extra," what is gratuitous, what does not fit into her practical world. She still has a peacock and two peahens, the remnant of a once-large flock that her first husband, the Judge, kept because they made him feel rich. Mrs. McIntyre has no appreciation of the birds whatsoever. Nevertheless, she does not actively attempt to get rid of them. Somewhat similarly, despite her threat to fire the Shortleys, she has never actually fired any of her unsatisfactory help; they have all left of their own accord. And, though she wants Mr. Guizac to leave, she cannot quite bring herself to fire him.

Mr. Shortley, who has returned and been rehired, is even more interested in getting rid of Mr. Guizac than Mrs. McIntyre is. Wanting to get back his old job in the dairy, which is now being done by Mr. Guizac, Mr. Shortley identifies the Pole with the Germans he fought in World War I, and complains about the injustice of his country's enemy being given his job:

"Gone over there and fought and bled and died and come back on over here and find out who's got my job—just exactly who I been fighting. It was a hand-grenade come that near to killing me and I seen who throwed it—little man with eye-glasses just like his [Guizac's]. Might have bought them at the same store. Small world," and he gave a bitter little laugh.

Finally, impatient with Mrs. McIntyre's reluctance to take action, Mr. Shortley brings about an "accident" in which Mr. Guizac is run over by a tractor and killed. Mrs. McIntyre saw what was about to happen and did not shout a warning, and thus is morally guilty of complicity in his death.

As a result of Mr. Guizac's death, Mrs. McIntyre's world is virtually destroyed. Her help leaves, she develops a "nervous affliction," and is unable to run her farm. Eventually she becomes voiceless, half-blind, and bedridden. All that is left of her world is the peacock and the two peahens, for which she never had any use in the first place, and the priest who had arranged for the Guizacs to come, who visits her once a week and explains—unasked—the doctrines of the Church. The story ends on this heavily ironic note: Mrs. McIntyre, who has all her life been so adamantly a practical, not a theological woman, is condemned to listen helplessly to religious instruction she has not asked to be given.

However, the symbolic use that O'Connor makes of Mr. Guizac and the peacock indicates that there is another level of meaning. Both he and the peacock are identified with Christ. "He didn't have to come at all," Mrs. McIntyre complained to the priest earlier in the story, referring to Mr. Guizac. "He came to redeem us," replied the priest, thinking of Christ. On a later occasion, impatient with the talk about Christ, Mrs. McIntyre dismissed it with the observation, "As far as I'm concerned, Christ was just another D.P."

As Mr. Guizac is "extra," the peacock is gratuitous; a peacock is of no use on a farm. O'Connor initially uses the bird's beauty to suggest the splendor of the created universe. The peacock's tail is described as being "full of fierce planets" and "small pregnant suns"; it is like a "map of the universe." Mrs. McIntyre sees this embodiment of the gratuitous beauty of the world in purely pragmatic and economic terms as "another mouth to feed." The priest, however, identifies the glorious bird with the glorified Christ. When he sees the peacock for the first time in full display, he bursts out, "The Transfiguration," referring to Christ's appearance before his disciples in dazzling glory. Mrs. McIntyre, O'Connor observes wryly, "had no idea what he was talking about."

The clear identification of the peacock and the Pole with Christ puts Mrs. McIntyre's response to them into a theological context; her indifference to the one and rejection of the other is, by extension, her attitude toward Christ. But the identification of the Pole and Christ works both ways; it not only establishes Mr. Guizac as a Christ figure, it also—

through Mr. Guizac's effect on Mrs. McIntyre's farm—says something about the effect of Christ on the world. Like Mr. Guizac, O'Connor intimates, Christ is felt to be the "extra," the one who does not fit in, the one who upsets the established order of things. Christ is the Displaced Person.

Like Christ, Mr. Guizac is rejected and killed, but his death, far from securing the way things were, destroys the old order. Mrs. McIntyre loses everything she was trying to preserve by getting rid of him. But the underlying symbolism of the story prevents the scene at the end from being simply one of irony and loss. The Pole—the humble, anonymous, suffering Christ—is gone, but the peacock, symbolizing the glorified Christ, remains to the end. Indeed, one suspects that the peacock, which has been at the farm longer than anyone else, including Mrs. McIntyre herself, will outlast them all.

"Good Country People," the penultimate story in the collection, is something of a comic variation on "A Good Man Is Hard to Find." As the grandmother of the title story thinks of herself as a good Christian woman who believes in all the conventional platitudes, Hulga Hopewell, the Ph.D. in philosophy who is the protagonist of "Good Country People," thinks of herself as a good nihilist who energetically disbelieves in all the conventional platitudes. In their titles both stories implicitly ask the reader to consider what are good men or good people. And in both stories O'Connor uses conventional language for comic and ironic purposes, emphasizing the meaninglessness of the platitudes in the mouths of her characters, and at the same time using their words to sound the main themes of the story. For instance, Hulga's mother, Mrs. Hopewell, characteristically strings together remarks like "Everybody is different. . . . It takes all kinds to make the world. . . . Nothing is perfect." Nevertheless, she actually tolerates differences and imperfections very poorly. Two of the themes in the story grow out of the characters' attitudes toward uniqueness ("everybody is different") and imperfection.

Mrs. Hopewell and her tenant's wife, Mrs. Freeman, embody contrasting ways of looking at the world that provide the frame for the story. Whereas Mrs. Hopewell is determined always to put a smiling face on things and never look beneath the surface, the gimlet-eyed Mrs. Freeman has a fondness for hidden things: "the details of secret infections, hidden deformities, assaults upon children." She is obsessed with the physical demands and ills of the body, and in her conversation about her two daughters she dwells on the details of two major aspects of their physical being: their sexuality and their ailments. One daughter, Glynese, is being courted by several admirers, one of whom is going to chiropractor school and who cures her of a sty by popping her neck. The other daughter, Carramae, is pregnant and unable to "keep anything on her stomach."

Mrs. Hopewell's daughter, Hulga, is antagonized by her mother's platitudinous optimism to the extent that her face has come to wear a look of constant outrage that "obliterated every other expression." She finds Mrs. Freeman tolerable only on the ground that Mrs. Freeman diverts some of her mother's attention from her; otherwise, she is uncomfortable with Mrs. Freeman's fascination with the secrets of the body.

Hulga has rejected the physical world and the life of the body in preference for the life of the mind: "She didn't like dogs or cats or birds or flowers or nature or nice young men. She looked at nice young men as if she could smell their stupidity." Her rejection of the physical world stems from her awareness of its liability to imperfection. Hulga's own imperfection is gross—she lost a leg when she was ten—but O'Connor obviously intended her to be a figure of all mankind, which suffers from the imperfections of the human condition. Hulga insists on calling attention to her physical imperfection and refuses to try to improve her appearance. However, this defensive insistence that she be accepted "LIKE I AM" does not indicate that *she* has really accepted what she is; rather, it suggests that she is trying to insulate herself against the pain of difference and imperfection.

Hulga's choice of her name reflects her response to her condition. Named Joy by her mother, she could not tolerate the incongruity between the idea of joy and her knowledge that she was "dust." She therefore chose to emphasize her deformity and ugliness by assuming an ugly name—Hulga—and a rude manner, and closed herself to joy for the sake of affirming the truth about herself. The persona she creates with the name Hulga is a blind, stony, armored creature. To her mother, the name Hulga suggests the "broad blank hull of a battleship." Hulga herself is described as being "square and rigid-shouldered," and as standing "blank and solid and silent." Her face is characteristically expressionless, and her "icy blue" eyes have the "look of someone who has achieved blindness by an act of will and means to keep it." Though she believes the self she has created is her true self, this imagery suggests that her willful blindness prevents her from seeing the true nature of the human condition as much as does her mother's insistence on always looking "at the bright side of things."

Though she has rejected joy for herself, Hulga has not given up on the possibility of love, and this secret desire is her one area of vulnerability. However, she thinks the persona she has created through her name is a means of making herself invulnerable, so that she can command and control love from a position of strength. She envisions her name working "like the ugly sweating Vulcan who stayed in the furnace and to whom the goddess [of love] had to come when called."

When an apparently naive country boy appears selling Bibles, Hulga feels that he offers no threat to her and allows herself to respond to his open admiration. Despite her utter inexperience (she has never been kissed) she decides to demonstrate her command of love by seducing him. She reinforces her image of herself as a woman of intellectual superiority and worldly wisdom by imagining that the simple Bible salesman, once seduced, will suffer from remorse, whereupon she will take away his shame and "transform it into something useful."

However, the Bible salesman's simplicity seduces her. Having climbed with her into the loft of an isolated barn, the Bible salesman gets Hulga to declare (with some reservations) that she loves him. He then demands that she prove it by showing him where her wooden leg joins on. At first shocked by his proposal, Hulga resists until he tells her why: "because [the wooden leg is] what makes you different." She feels that the Bible salesman, "with an instinct that came from beyond wisdom, had touched the truth about her." She comes to the conclusion that for the first time in her life she has encountered true innocence. She is so moved by her perception of his innocence that she lets down her defenses and allows her hidden vulnerability to emerge.

This area of vulnerability O'Connor equates with Hulga's soul and symbolizes it by her wooden leg: "she was as sensitive about the artificial leg as a peacock about his tail. No one ever touched it but her. She took care of it as someone else would his soul, in private and almost with her own eyes turned away." The leg is also, as the Bible salesman cannily recognized, what makes her different—a difference which, up to now, she has worn defensively and defiantly. Now, for the first time in the story, she accepts her difference, and allows herself to be touched in what is symbolically her soul. Accepting herself, she can surrender herself, and having surrendered herself she finds herself again, in the classic progression of love. When she allows the Bible salesman to remove her leg, "it was like surrendering to him completely. It was like losing her own life and finding it again, miraculously, in his."

Significantly, she surrenders to love in a scene in which her physical grotesqueness is not only emphasized but becomes the very means of love's expression and fulfillment. Though this scene of the Bible salesman removing Hulga's wooden leg is objectively ludicrous (and O'Connor's handling of it is full of irony), Hulga herself is, for the first time, completely without irony. The boy seems to her to be "entirely reverent" as he approaches the leg, and his removal of it is clearly the psychological and emotional equivalent to Hulga of the act of love: "She was thinking that she would run away with him and that every night he would take the leg off and every morning put it back on again."

Hulga's surrender to love also makes her vulnerable to a revelation of her own blindness. She had been convinced that she can see and that others cannot, and that she knows the truth. "Woman!" she had once shouted at her mother, enraged at Mrs. Hopewell's habit of blandly papering over ugliness with smiles. "Do you ever look inside ... and see what you are *not?*" As a philosopher, Hulga is professionally concerned with truth. She is convinced that she has no illusions, that she has seen through appearances to the nothing that is beneath. "Some of us," she informs the Bible salesman, "have taken off our blindfolds and see that there's nothing to see." And she is utterly convinced of the truth of her assessment of the Bible salesman's innocence.

The Bible salesman, however, is anything but an innocent. Having put Hulga's leg out of her reach, he takes out of his suitcase a hollowed-out Bible containing a flask of whiskey, a deck of pornographic playing cards, and a packet of contraceptives. In response to Hulga's evident dismay, he replies, "What's the matter with you all of a sudden? ... You just a while ago said you didn't believe in nothing. I thought you was some girl!" When he sees that he will get no farther with her, he snatches up her wooden leg, thrusts it into his suitcase, and disappears down the ladder of the barn loft.

The Bible salesman's thoroughgoing nihilism shows up Hulga's claim to believe in nothing as a superficial intellectual posture. Both his actions and his words devastate her assumption of intellectual superiority: "he turned and regarded her with a look that no longer had any admiration in it. ... 'And I'll tell you another thing, Hulga,' he said, using the name as if he didn't think much of it, 'you ain't so smart. I been believing in nothing ever since I was born!' "

Hulga is left stranded, her previously stony face "churning" with emotion. But the Bible salesman's destruction of her illusions and her defenses (like the destruction of conventional order that resulted from the grandmother's encounter with The Misfit) may be, for Hulga, the means of her salvation. That the Bible salesman might be a kind of savior is suggested in the description of Hulga's final glimpse of him. Looking out the window of the barn loft, she sees him making his way across the pasture. O'Connor implicitly compares him to Christ walking on the water; to Hulga's blurred vision (the Bible salesman has also taken her glasses), he seems to be "struggling successfully over the green speckled lake."

The actual or implied references to Christ in *A Good Man Is Hard to Find* are numerous. The climactic moment in the title story comes about after The Misfit expresses his intense concern over the question of whether or not Jesus raised the dead. Little Harry Ashfield in "The River" prefers the "Kingdom of Christ" where, he is told, he "counts," to his home where "everything is a joke." The image of the hermaphrodite in "A Temple of the Holy Ghost" is juxtaposed with the image of Christ in the Blessed Sacrament. The artificial nigger in the story of that name is implicitly a figure of Christ. Mr. Guizac in "The Displaced Person" is explicitly identified with Christ. The Bible salesman in "Good Country People" is implicitly compared to Christ.

Christ, as Simeon prophesied in St. Luke's gospel, is a

"sign that will be contradicted," a sign of the presence of God in the world that, to many, will not seem to be a sign of God at all—will seem, rather, its opposite. The unexpected and often grotesque and incongruous ways in which O'Connor felt Christ to be present in the world is, I think, the real subject of this collection. Not only is the image of Christ suggested in unlikely places or associated with unlikely characters; but in style as well the stories embody contradiction and incongruity—in the double point of view, in the mixture of comedy and horror, in the pervasive tone of emotional flatness and irony, on the one hand, and the intimations of depth and serious meaning on the other. Thematically and stylistically, the centrality of Christ—of that which we experience as contradictory—provides *A Good Man Is Hard to Find* with a unity that makes it more than simply a random collection of stories. Leon Driskell felt this unity and explained it (in *The Eternal Crossroads*) on the level of content, seeing Christ as the good man so hard to find who finally appears, in the person of Mr. Guizac, in the final story. To Driskell's interpretation I would add another gloss on the meaning of the title: the good man is so hard to find because he appears in such unlikely guises, because he is hidden in irony and contradiction.

3

•••

Everything That Rises Must Converge

The stories in O'Connor's second collection reflect her concern with questions implicitly raised by the rather gnomic title "Everything That Rises Must Converge." The phrase comes from the work of Pierre Teilhard de Chardin, a Jesuit paleontologist-philosopher. Teilhard hypothesized that evolution, far from stopping with the emergence of *homo sapiens*, continues to progress toward higher levels of consciousness, and that its ultimate goal is pure consciousness, which is Being itself, or God.

Teilhard's concept of the progress of evolution, actual and predicted, can best be visualized as a globe. At the base of the globe—the beginning of the evolutionary process—lines radiate outward and upward, representing the diversification of many forms of life which are moving upward toward greater levels of biological complexity. At the midpoint of the globe the diversification stops and one species—man—comes to dominate the earth. Moving from the midpoint of the globe upward, the lines begin to converge as they approach the topmost pole, the evolutionary destination that Teilhard called the Omega point. The converging lines now represent individual human consciousnesses which, as they rise, grow closer and closer together.

One aspect of this convergence can be seen in the increased intercommunication and interdependence of men in modern mass society. The increasingly complex interaction of men, Teilhard believed, tends to generate fresh bursts of evolutionary energy that produce still higher levels of consciousness, and these increases in consciousness find material expression in new technological breakthroughs. Teilhard, however, did not equate rising in consciousness solely with social or intellectual or scientific advances; he saw these achievements as manifestations of an increase in consciousness that was primarily a growing toward the fullness of Being—God—that is the source of all life.

O'Connor certainly regarded an increase in consciousness—which in her stories is signified by an increase in vision—to be a growing toward Being. However, her characters typically resist this kind of rising and the spiritual convergence with others that accompanies it. This has led some commentators to conclude that O'Connor's use of the title "Everything That Rises Must Converge" is largely, if not completely, ironic. (According to one critic, nothing rises in the title story but Julian's mother's blood pressure.[1]) It is true that O'Connor deliberately plays off the meaning of the title against numerous metaphors of non-convergent rising, and especially against her characters' desire to rise without convergence; for instance, the "rising" of Negroes is acceptable to Julian's mother only as long as there is no convergence: "they should rise, yes, but on their own side of the fence." The thrust of most of the stories, however, is to bring the protagonist to a vision of himself as he really is, and thus to make possible a true rising toward Being. That this rising is inevitably painful does not discredit its validity; rather, it emphasizes (as Teilhard's conception does not) the tension between the evolutionary thrust toward Being and the human warp that resists it—the warp which O'Connor would have called original sin.

Julian, the protagonist of the title story, considers the position in which he finds himself to be monumentally beneath his dignity. He is taking his mother, who is overweight and has high blood pressure, to her reducing class at the Y, because she will not ride the buses by herself at night now that they have been integrated. As he waits for her while she adjusts a hideous green and purple hat, he feels as if his sensibilities are suffering martyrdom; leaning against the door frame, he seems to be "waiting like Saint Sebastian for the arrows to begin piercing him."

A would-be intellectual, Julian likes to think that he has raised himself, by his own efforts, above his mother's anachronistic values and above the intellectual sterility of his environment. This rising implies no convergence. Although he has fantasies about making friends with Negroes (to express his liberal views and annoy his conventional Southern mother), he has no real desire for convergence with anyone. He thinks of himself in proud isolation from others, retreating into an "inner compartment" of his mind whenever "he could not bear to be a part of what was going on around him." His idea of an ideal home is one where the nearest neighbors are three miles away on either side.

Whatever signs of convergence of social classes or races are evident in the story are dealt with by the characters in ways that minimize any real meeting. Julian's mother believes she can "go anywhere"—i.e., mix in any kind of social situation—because she is a descendant of a once-proud family: "if you know who you are, you can go anywhere." When a Negro woman gets on the bus wearing a hat identical to her own, she is dismayed by this sign of identity between them. She handles the situation by reducing the other woman to a subhuman level and seeing the implied relationship between them as a comic impossibility: "She kept her eyes on the woman and an amused smile came over her face as if the woman were a monkey that had stolen her hat." She thinks the Negro woman's child is "cute," and attempts to give the little boy a "shiny new penny" as they get off the bus. The woman, outraged at this sign of white condescension, literally converges with her and batters her in the face with her enormous handbag. Julian's mother, knocked to the ground, suffers a stroke.

Thus far, the metaphors of rising and convergence in the story seem to be purely ironic. Julian's mother's death, however, does bring about a rising in consciousness in Julian, and the nearness of death brings her to a real desire for convergence with a beloved Negro nurse of her childhood. The motions of true rising in both characters come about through an apparent descent, a regression back to childhood. Julian, in the midst of an angry tirade at his mother, finally becomes aware of what is happening to her. Shocked out of his self-justifying and isolating "adult" behavior by this realization, he is precipitated back into his childhood love for her: " 'Mother!' he cried 'Darling, sweetheart, wait!' Crumpling, she fell to the pavement. He dashed forward and fell at her side, crying, 'Mamma, Mamma!' " She, too, regresses to childhood, calling out for her old Negro nurse Caroline to come and get her. Unable to accept the convergence of social equality with Negroes in life, she nevertheless turns to the memory of a Negro with a true motion of convergence as she is dying.

The shock of his mother's dying brings Julian not only into contact with his buried love for her but also to the verge of realizing his repeated betrayals and denials of that love. The story has an almost tragic force in its evocation of the horror attendant upon Julian's dawning discovery of his blindness of what he has been and done. His all-too-human reluctance to be fully illuminated, and the nature of the illumination that is awaiting him, are beautifully suggested in the final lines of the story. O'Connor describes him seeming to be swept back toward his mother, toward his childhood connection with her, by a "tide of darkness" that "postpon[es] from moment to moment his entry into the world of guilt and sorrow."

In "The Enduring Chill" O'Connor uses conventional religious imagery for comic purposes but finally reveals in the imagery an unexpected and terrifying reality. Asbury, the protagonist, is another would-be writer who believes himself to be far superior to the Southern environment in which he was raised. As the story opens, he has just come back from New York City to his mother's dairy farm, believing he has a fatal illness. Wanting to bring his mother to a realization of how her commonplace life has stifled his artistic talent, he plans to leave her a lengthy letter—"such a letter as Kafka had addressed to his father"—to be read after his death. His attitude toward death is full of romantic posturings; he believes that "he had failed his god, Art, but he had been a faithful servant and Art was sending him Death."

His life, too, is full of posturings. Before his illness he had attempted a ludicrous "communion" with the Negro hands on his mother's farm by smoking with them and trying to get them to share a glass of unpasteurized milk with him in the dairy. Now, convinced he is dying, he badgers his mother into sending for a Jesuit priest because he wants to talk to "a man of culture" and he believes Jesuits to be sophisticated and worldly, and also because he knows it will annoy his Methodist mother. The priest, who turns out to be Irish and orthodox, brusquely turns aside Asbury's attempts to initiate a literary discussion and (in one of the funniest scenes in the O'Connor canon) examines him on his catechism. Finding Asbury deplorably ignorant, he exhorts him to ask God to send him the Holy Ghost. Asbury, furious at this turn of affairs, retorts to the priest that "the Holy Ghost is the last thing I'm looking for!"

When his illness is finally diagnosed as undulant fever (which is recurrent but not fatal), contracted by drinking the unpasteurized milk, Asbury's pretentious illusions about himself suffer a terrible blow. Instead of a romantic death, he is condemned to the terrifying reality of living and seeing himself clearly for what he really is. His eyes look "shocked clean as if they had been prepared for some awful vision about to come down on him." As that vision comes, an image made by water stains on the ceiling above his head—which has seemed to Asbury since childhood to be a "fierce bird" with icicles hanging from its wings—seems suddenly to be in motion. O'Connor identifies the bird with the Holy Ghost, traditionally imaged as a dove and the agent of spiritual illumination:

Asbury blanched and the last film of illusion was torn as if by a whirlwind from his eyes. He saw that for the rest of his days, frail, racked, but enduring, he would live in the face of a purifying terror. A feeble cry, a last impossible protest escaped him. But the Holy Ghost, emblazoned in ice instead of fire, continued, implacable, to descend.

O'Connor uses allusions from classical mythology to suggest the deeper levels of meaning present in "Greenleaf." Even the names of the protagonist, Mrs. May, and her tenants, the Greenleafs, suggest the springtime of the world and the ancient rites of fertility associated with that season. Mrs. May's character, however, is in ironic contrast to her name, for there is nothing yielding, receptive, or springlike about her. She runs her farm with an "iron hand." She pits herself against her tenants, the Greenleafs, who embody for her all that is shiftless and irresponsible, who live "like the lilies of the field." She fears that Mr. Greenleaf will wear her down by sheer attrition if she doesn't keep her "foot on his neck all the time." She sees the "rising" of the Greenleaf boys (they now own a prosperous farm after being educated on the G.I. bill) as a threat of unwelcome convergence. "And in twenty years . . . do you know what those people will be?" she asks her sons. *"Society,"* she replies blackly. However, she consoles herself with the thought that "no matter how far they *go,* they *came* from that." "That" is slovenly, uncouth Mrs. Greenleaf, who conducts "prayer healings" in the woods, moaning and crying over buried newspaper clippings recounting the atrocities of the world. Mrs. May's rejection of *that*—all that is primitive, unsocialized, mysterious, power-ful—is even more adamant than her refusal to consider any offspring of the Greenleafs socially acceptable.

As is usual in the O'Connor canon, the mysterious, chthonic forces of nature are symbols of divinity, and Mrs. May's relentless resistance to these forces suggests that the primary convergence she is attempting to avoid is union with God. The specific embodiment of the divine in the story is a "scrub" bull belonging to the Greenleaf sons. The bull, who likes to "bust loose" (suggesting the uncontainable power of divinity), appears at the opening of the story eating a hole in the hedge outside Mrs. May's bedroom window. The hedge (like the wall of trees surrounding her property) is a symbol of the metaphoric walls behind which Mrs. May isolates herself, and the bull is a destroyer of such defenses. His symbolic role as divine lover is made quite explicit early in the story. Standing outside her window, he is likened to "some patient god come down to woo her." Crowned with a wreath of hedge that has slipped over his horns, he is also implicitly associated with the garlanded victim of ancient sacrifice.

The threat that the bull represents to Mrs. May is ex-pressed largely through sexual metaphors. On the naturalis-tic level, she is afraid that this "scrub" bull will get in with her well-bred dairy cows and "ruin the breeding schedule." She has the same fear in regard to the Greenleafs them-selves; she is afraid that her ill-tempered sons (who seem capable of doing anything in order to annoy her) will marry "trash" like Mrs. Greenleaf and "ruin everything I've done."

Basically, Mrs. May's fears of the bull and the Green-leafs represent her anxiety about the intrusion of that which is vaster than she into her well-controlled life; she is afraid of being overpowered, either by the forces of nature or those transcending nature. Inasmuch as both the bull and the Greenleafs symbolize these forces, Mrs. May directs all her energies to keeping both the bull and the Greenleafs under her control.

When the bull repeatedly breaks out of his pen, and the Greenleaf boys display no eagerness to come and get him, Mrs. May decides to make Mr. Greenleaf shoot him. She orders Mr. Greenleaf to get his gun and drive out to the pasture with her. When the bull runs into the woods, she sits on the front bumper of the car and waits for Mr. Greenleaf to drive the bull back into the pasture. When the bull—who does not like cars—comes out of the woods he gallops toward Mrs. May with "a gay rocking gait as if he were overjoyed to find her again." The imagery again suggests that the bull is both a lover and a destroyer of defensive walls. Charging toward her, he "buried his head in her lap, like a wild tormented lover. . . . One of his horns sank until it pierced her heart and the other curved around her side and held her in an unbreakable grip." The tree line surrounding the pasture—symbolic of her outermost wall of defense— now appears to her as a "dark wound in a world that was nothing but sky." That wound is analogous to the wound the bull makes in the wall of her body as he penetrates to the very core of her being—her heart.

This "convergence" with the bull and all he symbolizes brings Mrs. May to an overwhelming illumination: "she had the look of a person whose sight has been suddenly restored but who finds the light unbearable." The bull, the divine lover whose embrace is death to the walled-in and control- ling self, becomes the sacrificial victim as Mr. Greenleaf runs up and shoots him "four times through the eye." (The analogy between the bull and Christ, who is traditionally the divine Bridegroom as well as the sacrificial victim on the cross, is too close to be overlooked.) United with the bull in death, Mrs. May seems to accept her divine suitor; as the bull's huge body sinks to the ground, Mrs. May is pulled forward so that, loverlike, she seems to be "bent over whis- pering some last discovery into the animal's ear."

Even more than Mrs. May, old Mr. Fortune, the protagonist of "A View of the Woods," is determined to resist convergence. In the consequences of his resistance, O'Connor may be suggesting that convergence—with others and, ultimately, with God—is demanded of man, and his unrelenting refusal of it makes him experience what is potentially a source of joy as the pain of hell. This is hinted at in Mr. Fortune's response to the woods. The view of the woods, and the cow pasture that commands it, have much the same function as the bull in "Greenleaf." They embody something non-utilitarian and gratuitous, something charged with mysterious power. They appear under different aspects according to how they are regarded. To the Pitts children in the story, who love the pasture, it is "where we play," and the view of the woods is of immense importance. To old Mr. Fortune, who cannot see letting trees and a pasture stand in the way of progress, the woods embody an "uncomfortable mystery" that he finds distinctly unpleasant. As he stares at the woods at sunset, the red light of the setting sun makes it seem to him "as if someone were wounded behind the woods and the trees were bathed in blood." To his eyes, the vision of the woods is "hellish."

Mr. Fortune is an old man who sees the advent of "progress" in his rural neighborhood as a means of maintaining his position of dominance over his family. He is of the opinion that "[a]nyone over sixty years of age is in an uneasy position unless he controls the greater interest." When an artificial lake is created adjacent to his property, he is able to sell off lakefront lots, thus both strengthening his financial position and causing considerable pain to his despised son-in-law, Pitts, who farms the old man's land and wants to buy it himself. Mr. Fortune's attitude toward his family—with one exception—is that of enormous contempt. The one exception is his granddaughter, Mary Fortune Pitts, who bears a strong resemblance to him and whom he sees as an extension of himself.

Mr. Fortune has decided to sell the pasture in front of his house as a site for a gas station, partly in the expectation of seeing his rural environment grow into a modern town, and partly for the pleasure of annoying his son-in-law. To his surprise and consternation, Mary Fortune—who heretofore has always supported him in his enterprises—strenuously objects to the sale because "We won't be able to see the woods across the road." Moreover, she adds, "My daddy grazes his calves on that lot." The child's loyalty to her father infuriates the old man, partly because it is loyalty to someone other than himself and partly because it is given to Pitts, who, for no apparent reason, beats her. She inexplicably submits to these beatings, though she denies to the old man that they take place. She even boasts that "Nobody's ever put a hand on me and if anybody did, I'd kill him."

As her name suggests, Mary Fortune Pitts embodies the union of Fortune and Pitts. In addition to her physical resemblance to her grandfather, she shares his fascination with signs of progress, particularly the construction of a fishing club on the shores of the artificial lake. She is, however, (though Mr. Fortune would like to overlook this) also a Pitts, as is reflected in her name, in her intense commitment to the view of the woods, and in her loyalty to her father. To Mr. Fortune, the convergence of Fortune and Pitts is abhorrent. As Mary Fortune's stubborn loyalty to the view of the woods and her father's calf pasture makes the Pitts in her more apparent, Mr. Fortune attempts to force her to choose between them: "Are you a Fortune," he asks her, "or are you a Pitts? Make up your mind."

Mr. Fortune's rejection of the importance of the view of the woods, and his refusal to accept the Pitts in Mary Fortune, have dire consequences. O'Connor suggests the spiritual dimensions of those consequences in the way she describes Tilman, the man to whom Mr. Fortune sells the pasture. Tilman has a triangular face, very narrow green eyes, and a head that weaves "snake-fashion" above his

body. Tilman's serpentine appearance suggests that Mr. Fortune is completing a deal with the devil.

When the sale is concluded Mary Fortune bursts into
the room in a fury and begins hurling pop bottles at Tilman.
Mr. Fortune, appalled at her behavior, decides he has been
too lenient with her and takes her out in the woods to whip
her. However, she will not consent to be beaten by him; she
attacks him, overcomes him, and crows in triumph, "You
been whipped . . . by me . . . and I'm PURE Pitts." Mr. Fortune is so outraged to see "his own image" call itself Pitts
that he strikes her head against a rock, asserting "There's not
an ounce of Pitts in me." Having done literally what he
intended to do metaphorically—kill the Pitts in the child—
he suffers a fatal heart attack.

As he is dying he has a hallucinatory vision: he believes
he is running out of the mysterious and threatening woods
toward the artificial lake. When he reaches it he realizes that
he can go no further, for he has no boat and he cannot
swim. Only the trees, the very things he is trying to escape
from, seem able to move on beyond the lake: "On both sides
of him he saw that the gaunt trees had thickened into mysterious dark files that were marching across the water and
away into the distance." He himself is stopped at the shore
of the lake, the construction site where he had sat with Mary
Fortune and watched the yellow machines of progress eating
a hole in what had been a cow pasture. The hopelessness of
the situation to which his choices have brought him is suggested in the final line of the story:

He looked around desperately for someone to help him but the
place was deserted except for one huge yellow monster [an
earth-moving machine] which sat to the side, as stationary as he
was, gorging itself on clay.

In "The Comforts of Home" the action that starts the
story moving is an act of charity on the part of the protagonist's mother that represents a true movement toward con-

vergence: she has taken an amoral and incorrigible girl who calls herself Star Drake (née Sarah Ham) into the home she shares with her son Thomas. She undertakes this quixotic act of charity because, as she tells Thomas, "I keep thinking it might be you. . . . If it were you, how do you think I'd feel if nobody took you in? What if you were a nimpermaniac [sic] and not a brilliant smart person and you did what you couldn't help and. . . ." To Thomas, a good man devoted to order and moderation, being identified in any way with the "little slut" is insufferable; hearing his mother thus link his condition, even in the realm of remote possibility, with that of Sarah Ham, Thomas feels "a deep unbearable loathing for himself, as if he were slowly turning into the girl."

The motions toward convergence that are embodied in his mother's actions and attitudes are seen by Thomas, who is the point-of-view character, to be excessive, foolhardy, useless, and destructive of the peace of their home. And, though Thomas's outrage and frustration at the loss of his comforts of home are portrayed in a comic light, Thomas himself is presented as a character whose views it is possible to take seriously. His desire to get Sarah Ham out of the house seems eminently understandable and even justifiable, as does his furious refusal of any kind of convergence with her—whether that of ordinary politeness, or the convergence of the sexual encounter that she openly invites, or the spiritual convergence implied in his mother's repeated "it might be you."

Though Thomas's refusal of convergence with the girl grows out of his loathing for the corruption and moral disorder she embodies, his desire to get rid of her leads him to an undesired convergence with the evil spirit of his deceased father. Thomas had not been able to endure his ruthless and dishonest father when he was alive, but as his exasperation grows and his mother persists in her course of "daredevil charity," he remembers that his father would have put an end to any such nonsense before it got started. The voice of his father begins to rasp in his head: "Numbskull, the old man said, put your foot down now. Show her who's boss before she shows you." The evil nature of Thomas's father is suggested in the description of him taking up a squatting position in Thomas's mind; the image recalls that of Satan in Milton's *Paradise Lost*, squatting in the form of a toad at the ear of Eve.

Thomas initially resists the tempter's suggestions. "Several ideas for getting rid of her had entered his head but each of these had been suggestions whose moral tone indicated that they had come from a mind akin to his father's, and Thomas had rejected them." However, after Sarah Ham has been in the house for a week, during which time she has histrionically (and ineffectively) cut her wrists, entered Thomas's study in his absence and taken his gun from his desk drawer, and entered his bedroom unclothed at night, Thomas delivers an ultimatum to his mother: either the girl goes or he goes. When this does not work, he finally capitulates to his father's suggestions that he see the sheriff—a man "as easily dishonest" as his father—and get her arrested for stealing his gun.

Having arranged for the sheriff to come and search her room for the gun, Thomas returns home and finds, to his dismay, that the gun is back in his desk drawer where it belongs. Frantic, he gives in to his father's commands to plant it in her handbag. Caught in the act by the girl and accused by her in the presence of his mother, Thomas (prompted by the voice of his father) delivers a counter-accusation: "The dirty criminal slut stole my gun!" Furious, the girl lunges at him and Thomas, again responding to his father's promptings, fires. But his mother has thrown herself between them to protect the girl, and the shot kills her instead. At that moment the door opens and the sheriff, unnoticed by Thomas and the girl, surveys the scene. The story concludes with his interpretation of what he sees: "the fellow had intended all along to kill his mother and pin it on the girl.... As he scrutinized the scene, further insights were flashed to him. Over her body, the killer and the slut were about to collapse into each other's arms."

The convergence with the girl that Thomas was so determined to avoid is thus brought about by his own actions. This convergence is emphasized by the sheriff, who assumes a sexual relationship between Thomas and the girl and sees them, in addition, as partners in crime. In actual fact the sheriff's interpretation of the scene is grossly inaccurate—the furthest thing from Thomas's mind was to kill his mother, whom he loved, and embrace the detested girl; however, the sheriff's view does accurately manifest some important symbolic realities. Thomas's planting of his gun in the girl's purse is, symbolically, a sexual act; the phallic symbolism of the gun and the description of the "skin-like feel" of the purse—which, when opened, emits an odor of the girl—are only too obvious. He has thus symbolically united himself with her; moreover, he has also joined her (as the sheriff thought) in criminality, for Thomas's intent in planting the gun was plainly dishonest. He and the girl have not committed the same crime, but his actions have demonstrated that he is more like the girl than he has been willing to acknowledge. It is not true that he has "No bad inclinations, nothing bad [he was] born with."

In O'Connor's theological view, the "something bad" one is born with, which one cannot help, is original sin. O'Connor evidently felt that the man who is good by secular humanitarian or ethical standards tends to disbelieve in any inherent evil in himself; this she saw to be a major obstacle to a true rising in consciousness, to vision, and to true convergence. True rising, she implies, begins with the recognition of oneself as a non-privileged member of sinful and suffering humanity, and true convergence involves union with what is most despised.

Sheppard of "The Lame Shall Enter First" is, like Thomas, a man who disbelieves in the existence of evil in himself. Even more than Thomas, Sheppard disbelieves in

the reality of evil qua evil. In the course of counseling in-
mates at the reformatory, Sheppard comes across Rufus
Johnson, a 14-year-old delinquent with a record of malicious
mischief, an I.Q. of 140, and a club foot. Sheppard's explanation of Johnson's behavior is psychological: "His mischief
was compensation for the foot." Johnson—raised by a
fundamentalist grandfather—counters Sheppard's view with
his own uncompromising belief that he does what he does
because of Satan: "He has me in his power." Because of the
boy's superior intellectual capacity, Sheppard is eager to
"save" Johnson and to prove to him that he is "not evil" but
only "mortally confused."

Sheppard values intelligence, goodness, and the ameli-
oration of social ills. He is deeply disappointed in his own
son, ten-year-old Norton, who is mediocre in intellect and
uninterested in sharing what he has with poor children or
with the disadvantaged Johnson. What Sheppard does not
realize is that Norton, who has all the material advantages,
feels himself more radically disadvantaged than Johnson.
Norton's mother is dead and the boy's grief is inconsolable.
He fears he has irrevocably lost her, for Sheppard—
contemptuous of stories of heaven and hell, which he feels
are "for the mediocre"—has told him that she no longer
exists. Sheppard is incapable of grasping what the thought of
his mother's nonexistence means to Norton; when he tells
Norton about Johnson's disadvantages, he lists the fact that
Johnson's mother is in the penitentiary. At this Norton
breaks down and howls: " 'If she was in the penitentiary,' he
began in a kind of racking bellow, 'I could go to seeeeee
her.' " Later, when Johnson talks to Norton about heaven
and hell, Sheppard observes with disgust that Norton "would
rather she be in hell than nowhere." Sheppard's values are
thus shown to be inadequate to meet the needs of his son.
Indeed, his values cause him to reject his son and to commit
the betrayal of love that is high on O'Connor's list of major
sins.

If we look at Sheppard's values in terms of "rising" and

"convergence," we see that he values rising very highly indeed; he wants both Johnson and Norton to rise to high
levels of intellectual ability and social goodness. Imagistically, Sheppard's interest in rising is expressed in terms of
his particular ambition for the boys: he wants them to study
the stars through a telescope and rise to the heights of the
physical heavens in space travel. This intellectual rising,
however, implies no convergence. Similarly, Sheppard's conception of goodness leads to isolation rather than to convergence. He conceives of his goodness as an "armor of kindness
and patience" which protects him from Johnson's insults.
The image suggests that the effect of his goodness is to make
him insensitive to the reality of Johnson's malice, but also—
such being the nature of armor—to the reality of Norton's
grief and need for love.

Sheppard is convinced that he can save Johnson by the
force of his own goodness. Johnson, however, is equally
determined to prove to Sheppard that he, Johnson, is evil
and that Sheppard cannot save him. Part of Sheppard's pro-
gram to save Johnson involves getting him a new orthopedic
shoe. Though he allows himself to be fitted for the shoe,
when it is ready he refuses to accept it. His deformed foot in
its ugly, battered shoe is a visible symbol of his spiritual
condition, and he will not accept Sheppard's attempt to deny
the symbolic significance of the deformity by improving on
its physical appearance.

The breakdown of Sheppard's faith in his own goodness
and in his ability to be Johnson's savior is brought about
through Johnson's deliberate malice. Johnson continues to
commit acts of vandalism, though he at first denies them in
a malicious effort to get Sheppard to trust him. When Sheppard has been sufficiently taken in, Johnson flaunts his
crimes before him. Johnson also befriends poor Norton,
apparently with the intention of annoying Sheppard by
teaching the boy about heaven and hell and Jesus. Almost
certainly, however, in telling the grief-stricken Norton that
his mother is in heaven and that he, Norton, would go to

heaven if he were to die right now, Johnson is deliberately setting the child up to kill himself.

Johnson is motivated not only by sheer malice but by outrage at what he perceives to be Sheppard's violation of truth. Early in the story, when Norton had attempted to defend his father by saying he was good, Johnson burst out, "I don't care if he's good or not. He ain't *right!*" Later, when Sheppard was reasserting his determination to save him, claiming that the "good will triumph," Johnson retorted, "Not when it ain't true.... Not when it ain't right." Truth, for Johnson, is fundamentally religious: that there is a heaven and a hell, that the Bible is true, and that nobody is capable of saving him—when he gets ready to be saved—but Jesus.

Sheppard, however, is convinced that Johnson does not really believe these religious truths: "I flushed that out of your head in the reformatory. I saved you from that, at least." Johnson's final actions in the story grow out of his furious determination to prove to Sheppard that he does, indeed, believe them, and to confront Sheppard with the truth. Johnson commits another act of vandalism, allows himself to be caught, and demands to be taken to Sheppard. In the presence of the policemen who have brought him, Johnson declares that he committed his vandalism to "show up that big tin Jesus!... He thinks he's God.... The devil has him in his power." He asserts that a natural inclination to evil, not maladjustment, is at the root of his behavior. "I lie and steal because I'm good at it!" he shouts at Sheppard. "My foot don't have a thing to do with it."

Sheppard, pained, defends himself: "I did more for him than I did for my own child. I hoped to save him and I failed, but it was an honorable failure. I have nothing to reproach myself with." Sheppard's defense contains his own condemnation: "I did more for him than I did for my own child." Finally, hearing his words echoing in his ears, he sees the truth of what he is saying: "He had stuffed his own emptiness with good works like a glutton. He had ignored his own child to feed his vision of himself." The agent of this revelation is "the clear-eyed Devil, the sounder of hearts," whom he sees "leering at him from the eyes of Johnson." With this rising in consciousness, Sheppard experiences a true desire for convergence; he feels a "rush of agonizing love" for Norton and hurries to tell him "that he loved him, that he would never fail him again." Norton, however, has sought rising and convergence elsewhere; believing that he has seen his mother in the heavens through the telescope that Sheppard bought to interest the boys in space travel, Norton has hanged himself to get to heaven where she is, and Sheppard finds him dangling from the beam "from which he had launched his flight into space."

Mrs. Turpin, the protagonist of "Revelation," is, like Sheppard, convinced of her own goodness. Mrs. Turpin is a good Christian woman who looks after the poor, works for the church, and thanks Jesus effusively for making her what she is—and not "a nigger or white trash or ugly." Mrs. Turpin's failure of charity, despite her works of charity, is obvious as she sums up the other patients in the doctor's waiting room in which the story opens. Sizing up a "stylish lady" as one of her own kind and striking up a conversation with her, Mrs. Turpin reveals, through her words and thoughts, her interior judgements on the others present. Her veiled racism and social snobbery, her cheerful complacency, and her unabashed pride in her good disposition are too much for the stylish lady's daughter, a fat, scowling girl who has obviously had to suffer much of the same sort of thing from her mother. The girl responds to Mrs. Turpin's remarks with ugly looks until finally, provoked beyond endurance, she flings a book at Mrs. Turpin's head and lunges at her throat. "Go back to hell where you came from, you old wart hog," the girl whispers to her fiercely.

Hog imagery has already been introduced in the conversation between Mrs. Turpin and the stylish lady. Mrs.

Turpin mentioned the hogs she raises in a concrete-floored pig parlor. Responding to an unwelcome interruption by a "white-trash woman," who declares hogs to be "Nasty stinking things, a-gruntin and a-rootin all over the place," Mrs. Turpin coldly replied that her hogs are washed down every day with a hose and are "cleaner than some children I've seen." ("Cleaner by far than that child right there," [the "white-trash" woman's child] she added to herself.)

O'Connor uses hogs in this story (and elsewhere) as symbols of unredeemed human nature. As no amount of external cleanliness can fundamentally change hog nature, so no amount of external goodness can fundamentally change human nature, which, in O'Connor's view, is contaminated with evil—whether it be the consciously chosen evil of Johnson or the more subtle evil of pride and self-righteousness displayed by Sheppard and Mrs. Turpin.

Evil seems a strong word to apply to a character like Mrs. Turpin, who, for all her pride and complacency, is surely not a "bad" woman. Yet O'Connor obviously felt that Mrs. Turpin's belief in her own goodness was, if anything, more of an obstacle to the salvation of her soul than an outright commitment to evil. Thomas Merton reflects on this paradox: "Truly the great problem is the salvation of those who, being good, think they have no further need to be saved and imagine their task is to make others 'good' like themselves."[2]

Mrs. Turpin is at first shocked and indignant at the injustice of what has happened to her. Why should she, a hard-working, respectable, church-going woman, be singled out for such a message when there was "trash in the room to whom it might justly have been applied"? At the same time, however, Mrs. Turpin senses that the girl "knew her in some intense and personal way, beyond time and place and condition," and the message, unpleasant as it is, has for her the force of divine revelation.

After pondering the girl's words with increasing wrath

and indignation all afternoon, Mrs. Turpin marches down to the pig parlor on her farm and contemplates her hogs. "What do you send me a message like that for?" she demands of God. "How am I a hog and me both? How am I saved and from hell too?" She rails at God with increasing sarcasm until, with a final surge of fury, she roars, "Who do you think you are?" An echo of her own words comes back to her, like an answer, out of the silence.

Who does she think she is? The imagery surrounding this scene suggests that Mrs. Turpin considers herself the equal of God. The sun, that perennial symbol of God in O'Connor's fiction, seems comically obedient to Mrs. Turpin's presumption, and hangs over the tree line in an attitude almost exactly imitative of her own position on the fence of the pig parlor: "The sun was behind the wood, very red, looking over the paling of trees like a farmer inspecting his own hogs." While this image embodies Mrs. Turpin's assumption of the equality between her and God, it also suggests that the true relation between them is that God is the farmer, the world is His farm, and Mrs. Turpin is one of the "hogs"—humanity—at which He is gazing. His gaze—His light, symbolically the infusion of His grace into the world —is transforming; in the light of the setting sun the pigs are suffused with a red glow, and appear to "pant with a secret life." Mrs. Turpin, too, is touched by this transforming light, and life flows into her. "Like a monumental statue coming to life," she bends her head and gazes, "as if through the very heart of mystery, down into the pig parlor at the hogs."

The mystery of humanity, as O'Connor saw it, is that it is rooted in earth, yet bathed in God's light that fills it with secert life, the life of grace that is in no way dependent on worthiness or on the scale of human values Mrs. Turpin cherishes. The irrelevance of social values in the sphere of grace is manifested in the vision that is given to her as she lifts her eyes from the pigs and gazes at the purple streak in the sky left like a trail by the setting sun:

ıw the streak as a vast swinging bridge extending upward
the earth through a field of living fire. Upon it a vast
: of souls were rumbling toward heaven. There were whole
companies of white-trash, clean for the first time in their lives,
and bands of black niggers in white robes, and battalions of
freaks and lunatics shouting and clapping and leaping like frogs.
And bringing up the end of the procession was a tribe of people
whom she recognized at once as those who, like herself and
Claud [her husband], had always had a little of everything and
the God-given wit to use it right. . . . They were marching behind the others with great dignity, accountable as they had
always been for good order and common sense and respectable
behavior. They alone were on key. Yet she could see by their
shocked and altered faces that even their virtues were being
burned away.

For her to rise, to follow even at the end of the heaven-
bound procession, it is necessary for her virtues to be burned
away, for her to see herself as no more worthy of God's
grace than the Negroes and white trash and freaks and lunatics she habitually looks down upon. Good works, in
O'Connor's view, do not redeem; they only prevent Mrs.
Turpin from seeing that she shares in the poverty and limitation and evil proclivities common to all humanity. She is not
capable of lifting herself out of this condition by her own
efforts; indeed, her efforts to do so only compound evil by
making her think herself superior to others and thus rein-
forcing social inequality, pride, and complacency. "Rising"
comes about by grace, and by Mrs. Turpin's response of
openness to it. Appropriately enough, the instrument of
grace—the ugly girl who hurled a book at Mrs. Turpin's
head and declared that lady's kinship with hogs and hell—is
named Mary Grace.

In O'Connor's stories, a character's refusal of convergence with others is an externalization of a deeper refusal to
accept convergence with Being. A character's desire to remain autonomous and in control of things prevents his sur-

render to the transcendent—to that which is greater than he, which is uncontrollable, which is, in the words of "Parker's Back," "to be obeyed." Expressed in other stories in naturalistic symbols—the bull, the sun, the woods—in "Parker's Back," transcendent Being is embodied in the face of a Byzantine Christ that is tattooed on the back of the protagonist, O.E. Parker.

A man who is otherwise as "ordinary as a loaf of bread," Parker was stirred with a mysterious longing when, at the age of fourteen, he saw at a fair a man covered from head to foot with tattoos that formed "a single intricate design of brilliant color." This initial response of wonder to what is to Parker a thing of beauty makes him literally a marked man, for ever afterward he has been subject to an unrest that can be assuaged only by the acquisition of a new tattoo. However, the total effect, on him, is "not of one intricate arabesque of colors but of something haphazard and botched."

Parker's frustrated longing for the perfection of aesthetic form grows more acute as the space on the front of his body is used up and the single, intricate effect is not achieved. His dissatisfaction provokes him to actions he does not understand, notably his marriage to Sarah Ruth Cates, the daughter of a Straight Gospel preacher. Sarah Ruth, a plain-looking woman, thinks his tattoos are a "heap of vanity." She spends most of her time telling him "what the judgement seat of God will be like for him if he doesn't change his ways."

Though he is unimpressed with Sarah Ruth's religious convictions, Parker is driven to consider getting a tattoo with a religious subject in order to get Sarah Ruth to look at it. Parker feels strongly that his tattoos are to be looked at. To have a tattoo on his back, where he cannot see it, seems to him sheer foolishness if Sarah Ruth will not look at it either. It is against her religion, however, to contemplate anything in the natural world as a sign or symbol of the transcendent; to do so, she thinks, is idolatrous. To her way of thinking, religion is entirely spiritual, entirely disembodied.

In O'Connor's view, however, the natural world is the medium of divine revelation. Thus when Parker, preoccupied by his need for a new tattoo and unable to think of one "that will bring Sarah Ruth to heel," runs his tractor into a big tree in the middle of a hayfield, the result is not simply a comic catastrophe but an event with supernatural significance. Parker is knocked out of his shoes and the tree bursts into flame. The flaming tree is implicitly for Parker what the burning bush was for Moses: a manifestation of the divine Presence. Struck with holy terror, Parker crawls backward toward his truck and drives straight to the city and to the tattoo parlor. There, trembling, he picks out the head of a Byzantine Christ with "all-demanding eyes" to be tattooed on his back.

The image of Christ on his back has literally the effect of a sacrament; though it is a symbol, it acts on Parker as if it were Christ Himself. Parker seeks out his pool-hall buddies but, unable to take their friendly razzing about his new tattoo, he gets into a fight and finds himself thrown out into the alley. O'Connor compares the pool hall, and the "nerve-shattering" calm that descends on it after Parker's ejection, to the ship "from which Jonah had been cast into the sea." The comparison suggests that Parker's motive in going to the pool hall in the first place was, like Jonah's, an attempt to evade a prophetic mission. Jonah had been called by God to preach to the city of Nineveh. Parker's prophetic mission is not so specific, but he does have a prophetic name—Obadiah Elihue—which he has kept a secret, using only the initials O.E.

Sitting in the alley outside the pool hall, Parker inspects his soul, the depths of his being that he had thought "was not at all important to him but which appeared to be necessary in spite of his opinion." His soul is in the process of being transformed from a "spider web of facts and lies" to "a single intricate arabesque of brilliant color" by the image of Christ that is now forever on his back.

That Parker is becoming a "new man" in Christ is emphasized in the description of his trip home: "It was as if he were himself but a stranger to himself, driving into a new country though everything he saw was familiar to him, even at night." Moreover, his attitude toward Sarah Ruth has changed radically; from wondering, in the opening of the story, why he had married her in the first place and why he did not leave her in the second, he comes to look to her as a source of guidance, and to want to please her. Bewildered at the effect the "all-demanding eyes" of the Christ on his back are having on him, he drives home to Sarah Ruth, confidently expecting that she "would know what he had to do . . . and she would at least be pleased. It seemed to him that, all along, that was what he wanted, to please her."

When he arrives home, Parker finds the door barricaded against him. When he identifies himself as O.E., Sarah Ruth denies she knows any O.E. and demands to know who he is. Just as the sun comes up, shooting a "tree of light" (reminiscent of the earlier tree of flame) over the horizon, Parker answers that he is "Obadiah Elihue." All at once he feels the light (here, as in "Revelation," a symbol of divine grace) pouring through him, "turning his spider-web soul into a perfect arabesque of colors, a garden of trees and birds and beasts." Sarah Ruth, however, is unmoved by the new tattoo that has accomplished the transformation of the designs on his body from "something haphazard and botched" into an aesthetic unity. When Parker tells her that the tattoo is a picture of God, she is outraged. " 'Idolatry!' Sarah Ruth screamed. 'Idolatry! . . . I can put up with lies and vanity but I don't want no idolator in this house!' " She picks up a broom and proceeds to beat Parker on the back "until she had nearly knocked him senseless and large welts had formed on the face of the tattooed Christ. Then he staggered up and made for the door."

In this image O'Connor graphically conveys the suffering of Christ incarnate in humanity, and expresses her belief that convergence with Christ means union with Christ's suffering, not escape from suffering into some abstract realm of spiritual bliss. And here also, as in the title story, Flannery O'Connor emphasizes that the rising in consciousness that precedes true convergence is expressed not through an increase in external power or dominance over others but, paradoxically, in a descent into vulnerability, into suffering, into weakness, into man's essential poverty. The story concludes with the image of the prophet, Obadiah Elihue, having been driven out of the house by his harridan wife, "leaning against the tree, crying like a baby."

In the last three stories in this collection, O'Connor began to go beyond the point at which, heretofore, she had characteristically ended her stories: the violent conclusion that implicitly contained a revelation capable of bringing the protagonist to see himself as he really is. "Revelation," the third from the last story, is transitional; the story continues, after Mary Grace's violent attack on Mrs. Turpin, to explore Mrs. Turpin's struggle to respond to the girl's message, but it does not go beyond Mrs. Turpin's tacit acceptance of the vision of herself bringing up the rear of the horde of souls trooping into heaven. What happens to a character after that acceptance is suggested in "Parker's Back"; Parker accepts the Christ on his back and his prophetic name, and the unexpected result is that he finds himself beaten and weeping underneath a tree. He has begun, the imagery suggests, to participate in the sufferings of Christ.

In "Judgement Day," the last story in the collection, old Tanner, the protagonist, has begun before the story opens to accept a convergence with the lowly and the suffering, symbolized by his relationship with his Negro friend Coleman. In old Tanner's situation O'Connor suggests that acceptance of convergence inevitably brings one "down" in the world—down into helplessness, into suffering, into the lot of

the most disadvantaged members of humanity. At the opening of "Judgement Day" old Tanner is already reduced to a
state of childlike weakness and dependency. Enfeebled by a
stroke, he is living in unhappy exile with his daughter in her
New York City apartment. In the course of the action he
experiences violent rejection, suffering, and finally death. His
death is not a means by which a revelation of something he
had vigorously resisted is forced upon him, as is the case in
most of the earlier stories in this collection. Rather, it is the
means of completing, both literally and symbolically, the
journey "home" that he was determined to set out on at the
beginning of the story.

"Home" is one of the dominant images in the story.
Literally, it is Corinth, Georgia, where old Tanner lived all
his life until his "high and mighty" daughter found him
living in a shack with his Negro friend Coleman. Scan-
dalized that he had come to "settle in with niggers," she
urged him to come and live with her in New York City.
Despite the fact that her opinion of his living situation
"shamed" him, Tanner might not have gone with her had he
not, that same day, discovered that the land on which he and
Coleman had built their shack had been bought by a pom-
pous Negro doctor. The doctor, Foley, let him know that if
Tanner wanted to stay, he would have to accept a reversal of
the traditional Negro-white roles. Unwilling to operate a still
for the doctor and be "a nigger's white nigger," Tanner had
gone north with his daughter. Once in New York, however,
he regretted his choice: "If he had known it was a question
of this—sitting here looking out of this window all day in
this no-place, or just running a still for a nigger, he would
have run the still for the nigger." He was not in New York a
week before he had decided to take the bus back to Georgia
as soon as his next monthly pension check arrived.

Before Tanner's check arrived, a Negro moved into the
apartment next door. Tanner's daughter warned him not to
"go over there trying to get friendly with him." In the

crowded city "convergence" is a physical reality, but "all stripes of foreigner" living together in a "pigeon-hutch" of an apartment building does not bring spiritual convergence. Tanner's daughter expresses what O'Connor felt to be the urban secular refusal of convergence: "you mind your business and they'll mind theirs. That's the way people were meant to get along in this world."

Tanner, however, lonesome himself and confident that "the nigger would like to talk to someone who understood him," waited for his new neighbor in the hallway and tried to make friends with him. To the city-bred Negro, however, Tanner's style of friendliness smacked of white patronage. Enraged at Tanner's repeated approaches, and at Tanner's addressing him as "Preacher" (the Negro is an actor and an atheist), he slammed the old man against the wall. The assault gave Tanner a stroke, and the medical expenses ate up his pension check.

Thus prevented from getting home on his own power, Tanner made his daughter promise to have him shipped home to Georgia when he dies. Relieved, he slept peacefully for a while and dreamed of arriving home in his coffin and surprising his friends, Coleman and Hooten the station agent, by springing up and shouting, " 'Judgement Day! Judgement Day! Don't you two fools know it's Judgement Day?' " As this fantasy indicates, Tanner equates "home," with all its particulars (Corinth, Coleman, Hooten), with heaven on the Day of Judgement, when the dead will be raised and the just will live eternally with God. Judgement Day is thus the equivalent of Teilhard's "Omega point," at which all created consciousness will be united with Being itself, with God.

Tanner's daughter, however, had no intention of keeping her promise. When Tanner learned of this—he overheard her telling her husband that she would have the old man buried in New York—he made up his mind to get home himself, "dead or alive." When the story opens, he is

waiting for his daughter to go out shopping so that he can
slip out of the apartment, hire a cab to take him to the train
yards, and get aboard a southbound freight. He has written a
note and pinned it in his pocket: "IF FOUND DEAD SHIP
EXPRESS COLLECT TO COLEMAN PARRUM, CORINTH, GEORGIA."
Barely able to walk, he gets as far as the head of the stairs
before his legs fail him and he pitches down the steep stair-
case. He is found there by the Negro actor and his disdainful
wife. Believing that he has reached home and that the coffin
containing his body is being unloaded from the train, Tanner murmurs, "Coleman?" The Negro actor interprets this
as a contemptuous epithet—"coal man"—and, mocking the
old man, he pulls Tanner's hat down his over his face and
thrusts his head and arms through the spokes of the ban-
nister.

This violent convergence with a hostile Negro on the
physical level brings about, on the spiritual level, a convergence with "otherness"—what is not oneself, and especially
what is feared and despised as alien and inferior. Tanner's
final convergence with the "negative image of himself" is
suggested through the position of his body on the stairs.
That position recalls an image that had come to him thirty
years before, when he first met Coleman. Then he had been
a lone white man bossing a team of unruly Negroes at an
isolated sawmill. A man with a reputation for being able to
"handle" Negroes, Tanner disarmed the half-drunk and potentially dangerous Coleman by whittling a pair of spectacles
out of a piece of bark and giving them to him:

> "What you see through those glasses?"
> "See a man."
> "What kind of a man?"
> "See the man make theseyer glasses."
> "Is he white or black?"
> "He white!" the Negro said as if only at that moment was
> his vision sufficiently improved to detect it. "Yessuh, he white!"
> he said.
> "Well, you treat him like he was white," Tanner said.

The spectacles enabled Coleman to "see" and accept Tanner in the traditional white man's role; but they also gave Tanner a momentary glimpse of a different vision. When Coleman put them on and looked at him and

grinned, or grimaced, Tanner could not tell which. . . . he had an instant's sensation of seeing before him a negative image of himself, as if clownishness and captivity had been their common lot. The vision failed him before he could decipher it.

The subsequent events of Tanner's life brought him increasingly closer to realizing that "common lot." He lost his property and lived with Coleman on terms of at least economic equality in the shack they built together. Then, in New York, he became willing to accept the reversal of traditional roles and work for the Negro doctor. Finally, in the circumstances of his death, he takes on the traditional Negro posture of "clownishness and captivity." The position of his body in death is that of a man confined and offered up to public mockery: his feet dangle over the stairwell "like those of a man in the stocks."

This is apparently an image of total defeat. Tanner has not got where he was going. The atheistic Negro has derided Tanner's belief in Judgement Day as the day of the resurrection of the dead and has asserted that the only judgement day is the day of death: "Ain't no judgement day, old man. Cept this. Maybe this here judgement day for you." Tanner's daughter carries out her intention to have him buried in New York. Yet the concluding paragraph of the story suggests that out of these apparent defeats, Tanner has achieved the ultimate convergence. After his daughter has had him buried, she cannot sleep at night, and she finally has him dug up and shipped to Corinth. That Tanner does, at last, arrive at his literal home suggests that he also arrives at his ontological home, union with God, imaged in the story as heaven on Judgement Day.

4

•••

Wise Blood

For a first novel, Wise Blood is strong and strikingly original. But the world of *Wise Blood* is a bizarre one, and the
novel's starkness of style and flatness of characterization, for
all that they are a part of the overall meaning and contribute
to its effect, prevent the novel from being easily accessible.
The world of *Wise Blood* is its own place, and makes few con-
cessions to our expectations of what a novel—especially one
that claims to be a comic novel—should be like. Rather, it
demands that we take it on its terms, and if we are willing to
do this, it unfolds for us a laconic, deadpan comedy that can
be simultaneously appalling and funny, a comedy that for all
its starkness has a terrible strength. Miles Orvell has noted
the cinematic quality of its images;[1] if it could be translated
with absolute fidelity to the screen, it would, I think, be
more immediately effective than it is as a novel.

As *Wise Blood* opens, the protagonist, Hazel Motes, is
en route to the city of Taulkinham on a train. Just dis-
charged from the army, Haze had first gone back to his
home town of Eastrod, Tennessee, but had found it completely abandoned. He is going to the city to look for a
"place to be." Haze is a bizarre figure wearing a "glare-blue"
suit with the price tag ($11.98) still attached and a "fierce"
hat like the kind worn by country preachers. His behavior is
definitely odd, and it is presented through a narrative that

focuses primarily on actions and provides few explanations of motives.

Three themes emerge from Haze's behavior on the train: his concern with the subject of "home," his intensely negative interest in the subject of Jesus and redemption, and his fear of death. He repeatedly accosts the Negro porter, whom he believes to be a "Parrum nigger" from his home town, Eastrod, despite the porter's surly avowals that he is from Chicago. His conversation with the loquacious Mrs. Wally Bee Hitchcock is a parody of the meaningless conversations that occur between strangers; however, Mrs. Hitchcock's conventional conversational gambits are laden with references to home.

To both Mrs. Hitchcock and the women with whom he shares a table in the dining car, Haze harps on his refusal of Jesus and redemption: "I reckon you think you been redeemed," he tells the startled Mrs. Hitchcock. "If you've been redeemed," he announces to the women in the dining car, "I wouldn't want to be.... Do you think I believe in Jesus? ... Well I wouldn't even if He existed. Even if He was on this train."

Haze's fear of death is evoked in his half-dreaming fantasies of the burials of his relatives as he lies that night in his coffinlike berth. He imagines each of his relatives intends to refuse death by refusing to let his coffin be shut on him; but in the end the coffin is shut, and the person inside does not make a move. Thus he dreams of his father's burial:

He saw him humped over on his hands and knees in the coffin, being carried that way to the graveyard. "If I keep my can in the air," he heard the old man say, "nobody can shut nothing on me," but when they got his box to the hole they let it drop down with a thud and his father flattened out like anybody else.

Juxtaposed with Haze's dreams of his relatives' deaths are memories which provide a partial explanation of the source of his attitude toward Jesus. The grandson of a circuit-riding preacher who had "Jesus in his head like a stinger," Haze grew up believing that he was going to be a preacher also. His grandfather's preaching emphasized the tenacity of Jesus, who "would die ten million deaths before He would let him [Haze] lose his soul, ... [who] would chase him over the waters of sin." Haze feared this "soul-hungry" Jesus and wanted only to avoid him. A good part of his fear stems from fear of the unknown. Haze imagines Jesus moving "from tree to tree in the back of his mind, a wild ragged figure motioning him to turn around and come off into the dark where he was not sure of his footing, where he might be walking on the water and not know it and then suddenly know it and drown." He wants the safety of what is known and predictable: "Where he wanted to stay was in Eastrod with his two eyes open, and his hands always handling the familiar thing, his feet on the known track, and his tongue not too loose."

Haze very early came to the conclusion that "the way to avoid Jesus was to avoid sin." If, as he had been taught, Jesus died to redeem him from sin, then if he avoided sin he was not in need of redemption, and thus was free of Jesus. After he was drafted into the army, however, his buddies told him that he had no soul, and he "converted to [a belief in] nothing." If he had no soul, there was nothing for Jesus to redeem and Jesus could have no claim on him.

This, then, is Haze's condition: he has no home in the world, and he is fiercely committed to the belief that he has no soul. Haze's first actions when he arrives in the city the following day grow out of his need of a home and his need to prove the nonexistence of his soul by asserting his disbelief in the reality of sin. His way of proving "that he didn't believe in sin" is to practice "what was called it." Thus the first thing he does is to go to a prostitute, Leora Watts. "Make yourself at home," she invites him, and further emphasizes the grotesque parody of "home" she offers by referring to him as "son" and herself as "Momma."

O'Connor repeatedly describes Haze's need of a home as need of a "place to be." Given her conviction that God is the ground of one's being, one's spiritual "place to be," as it were, it seems obvious that Haze's literal homelessness is a metaphor for the spiritual homelessness that is a result of his denial of spiritual realities. (Later in the novel he asserts, "Nothing matters but that Jesus don't exist," and declares that "it was not right to believe in anything you couldn't see or hold in your hands or test with your teeth.")

Despite his protestations of disbelief in Jesus, Haze is nevertheless obsessed with him. Exploring the city, he meets a friendless boy named Enoch Emery, who attaches himself to Haze, and a fake blind preacher named Asa Hawks and his fifteen-year-old daughter, Sabbath Lily. Haze (who repeatedly asserts his ability to "see") takes Hawks for what he appears to be. Hawks claims to have blinded himself with lime "to justify his faith in Jesus." Haze is fascinated with the scars on his face and with the eyes that are hidden behind dark glasses; much of the action of the novel stems from his gravitation toward Hawks and his attempt to see "*behind* the black glasses." (It seems clear from Haze's behavior that he is secretly convinced that Hawks can see something that he, Haze, cannot.) Moreover, it is in response to Hawks (who shoves a stack of religious tracts into Haze's hands and tells him to distribute them to the passing crowd) that Haze begins preaching. At first he merely warns the passers-by to avoid the blind "fool down there giving out tracts." Then, warming to his occupation, he begins to preach *his* version of the way things are:

Maybe you think you're not clean because you don't believe. Well you are clean, let me tell you that. Every one of you people are clean and let me tell you why if you think it's because of Jesus Christ Crucified you're wrong. I don't say he wasn't crucified but I say it wasn't for you. Listenhere, I'm a preacher myself and I preach the truth. . . . Don't I know what exists and what don't? . . . Don't I have eyes in my head? Am I a blind man?

Haze returns to Mrs. Watts, but concludes that she does not offer him a satisfactory "place to be." He leaves and buys himself an old "rat-colored" car to be his home, his means of transportation, and his pulpit, all in one. Though the car is obviously a wreck, he has enormous faith in it; he repeatedly pronounces it to be a "good car" that will take him wherever he wants to go. He literally takes his stand on it, preaching to passers-by of his new "Church Without Christ" while standing on the nose of the car. His gospel of nothing is expressed in negations of traditional religious doctrines:

there was no Fall because there was nothing to fall from and no Redemption because there was no Fall and no Judgement because there wasn't the first two.

He calls for a "new kind of jesus . . . one that can't waste his blood redeeming people with it, because he's all man and ain't got any God in him."

Haze's call for a new jesus is heard by Enoch Emery, the friendless boy he met on his first night in Taulkinham. Enoch's activities in the novel are an inverted parody of Haze's. Whereas Haze repudiates the redeeming blood of Jesus, Enoch believes fervently in the "wise blood" he believes he has inherited from his daddy. (Enoch even claims that his daddy "looks just like Jesus" because of his long hair.)

Enoch's world is a thoroughly naturalized world that has no vestige of spirit in it. A guard at the zoo, Enoch hates and envies the animals because—for all that they live in "a long set of steel cages like Alcatraz Penitentiary"—he feels that their existence is more comfortable than his: "The cages were electrically heated in the winter and air-conditioned in the summer and there were six men hired to wait on the animals and feed them T-bone steaks." Outside of his attempts to make friends with Haze, Enoch's efforts at human relationships are largely confined to watching women at the zoo's swimming pool from behind a clump of bushes and exchanging insulting remarks with waitresses.

Despite the grotesque naturalism of Enoch's world, Enoch has a primitive religious response to "mystery." When he came to the city he instinctively sought out the heart of things, the local equivalent of the sacred *omphalos*, the navel of the earth; he went to the literal heart of the city, which happened to be the zoological gardens. At the "heart of the park" he found a "mystery" that "so stunned and awed and overwhelmed [him] that just to think about it made him sweat." This "mystery" is a three-foot-long shrunken mummy of a man in a glass case in the museum. Every day Enoch performs an unconscious parody of religious ritual leading up to veneration of the mummy in the glass case.

Enoch's "wise blood" leads him to other actions that are parodies of elements in traditional religion. Blindly following the instruction of his blood (a parody of faith), Enoch finds himself cleaning his room and putting it in readiness for something. The central object of his concern in the room is his washstand. This object has a lower portion, described as a "tabernacle-like cabinet," meant to contain a slop jar. Enoch is led to paint the inside of the cabinet with gilt paint. The description of the cabinet invites its comparison to the tabernacle in which, in the Catholic church, the consecrated Host which is the Body of Christ is reserved.

When, having prepared the "tabernacle," he hears Hazel Motes call for a "new jesus," Enoch knows at once that the "new jesus" is the mummy in the glass case, and knows "that he had a place in his room prepared to keep it in until Haze was ready to take it." Once he has stolen the mummy, however, his attitude toward it—originally fear and awe—becomes mixed with resentment because the thing he believed was going to happen to him as a result of doing what his wise blood told him to do does not happen as he expects it. His expectation is a parody of the Christian belief that the "old man" is transformed, through faith, into a

"new man" in whom Christ lives. Thus, expecting a transformation, Enoch "pictured himself . . . as an entirely new
man, with an even better personality than he had now."
Disgruntled when nothing happens, Enoch sullenly delivers
the mummy to Haze. But he cannot get over the expectation
"that the new jesus was going to do something for him in
return for his services."

Enoch's ambition is for fame and admiration; "he
wanted, some day, to see a line of people waiting to shake
his hand." He reads in the newspaper that Gonga, the gorilla
movie star, is making a personal appearance at a local theater. Gonga's personal appearances consist of his standing
outside a theater and shaking the hands of the patrons.
Enoch has already had an encounter with him; he was in-
sulted by the man inside the gorilla suit when, in addition to
shaking the gorilla's hand, Enoch began to tell him all about
himself. Now Enoch sees his chance to attain his ambition
and to revenge himself on Gonga as well. Armed with a
sharp-pointed umbrella shaft, he makes his way to the theater and slips into Gonga's truck while Gonga is busy shaking hands. After Gonga and his managers drive away there
is a scuffle in the back of the truck, from which a somewhat
battered Enoch slips out, carrying the gorilla suit and apparently leaving the former inhabitant of the suit dead or
wounded. Enoch buries his own clothes and "disappear[s]"
into the gorilla suit. The new gorilla practices growling,
beats its chest, and extends its hand to be shaken.

Enoch has realized his ambition and is in bliss:

No gorilla in existence, whether in the jungles of Africa or Cali-
fornia, or in New York City in the finest apartment in the
world, was happier at that moment than this one, whose god had
finally rewarded it.

The "reward" that the new jesus offers is, literally, a transformation into bestiality. Seeing a courting couple sitting on
a rock overlooking a view of the distant city, Enoch the

gorilla advances toward them, hand extended. They flee, terrified, and Enoch is last seen in the novel sitting on a rock, staring out "over the valley at the uneven skyline of the city."

Haze, meanwhile, has kept up his pursuit of Hawks. He has located the rooming house where Hawks and his daughter live and has taken a room there himself. He expects that Hawks will try to save his soul, and is nonplused when Hawks shuts his door in Haze's face. Haze then decides to seduce Hawks's child: "He thought that when the blind preacher saw his daughter ruined, he would realize that he [Haze] was in earnest when he said he preached The Church Without Christ."

Haze assumes that Hawks's daughter is innocent because she is a preacher's daughter and because she is "so homely." Actually, she is lecherous for Haze and (as she tells him later) "pure filthy right down to the guts." He soon gives up on the idea of seducing her and tries to protect himself from her aggressive pursuit of him, but he fails to see that she is not innocent and that her father is not what he appears to be. When she lets him know that she is a bastard, Haze's only response is bafflement that her father—a preacher—could have had a bastard child. Finally, one night, he picks the lock on Hawks's door in order to get a close look at the blinded eyes while Hawks is sleeping. When Haze strikes a match, Hawks opens his eyes and stares at him. Expressionless, Haze leaves.

Haze's discovery that the blind man is not blind is his first revelation that his much-vaunted ability to see what is real leaves something to be desired. The following night he finally is made to see that Sabbath Lily is not innocent when he comes back to his room and finds her established in his bed. But there are still some things that Haze resists seeing, even though they are plainly shown him. First of all, he is given the "new jesus" he has called for, but he rejects it violently.

The morning after Sabbath Lily took up residence in Haze's bed, Enoch Emery arrives to give the new jesus to Haze. It is intercepted by Sabbath Lily, who mockingly presents it to Haze as their child. The image that Sabbath Lily makes, standing in the doorway holding the mummy, is a parodic echo of the Virgin and the child Jesus. This new jesus fulfills the specifications that Haze had called for: dried and stuffed, it "can't waste [its] blood redeeming people with it, because [it's] all man and ain't got any God in [it]." When Haze sees the new jesus, however, it appears that he does not like it; he smashes it against the wall, and throws the dusty remains out into the rain.

Haze is then shown an image of himself preaching in the person of Solace Layfield, the hired "prophet" of a competitive Holy Church of Christ Without Christ, set up by a religious con artist named Hoover Shoats. Layfield wears a "glare-blue" suit and "fierce" hat like Haze's, and standing on the nose of an identical high "rat-colored" car, he preaches a parody of Haze's parody of the Gospel: "The unredeemed are redeeming theirselves and the new jesus is at hand!"

Haze perceives that Layfield believes in Jesus even though Layfield claims he does not. Since Layfield is literally a mirror image of Haze, he suggests to Haze (and to the reader) that Haze, too, believes in Jesus even though he claims he does not. Haze immediately identifies Layfield as his "conscience"—though, at the same time, he asserts that a conscience is merely an illusion:

"Your conscience is a trick," he said, "it don't exist though you may think it does, and if you think it does, you had best get it out in the open and hunt it down and kill it, because it's no more than your face in the mirror is or your shadow behind you."

Haze thereupon proceeds to "hunt ... down and kill" Layfield, the embodiment of his conscience. Following him after Layfield's evening stint of preaching, Haze rams Layfield's car on a lonely road and pushes it into a ditch. To Layfield's bewilderment, Haze demands of him, "What do you get up on top of a car and say you don't believe in what you do believe in for?" He runs Layfield down and backs his car over him, thus both killing the "conscience" he professes to disbelieve in and killing the part of himself that says it doesn't believe in Jesus. (That he also commits murder is, to the alienated Haze, irrelevant. To him, the killing of Layfield is in the same category as smashing the mummy.)

Having decided to leave Taulkinham and preach The Church Without Christ in a new city, Haze stops at a gas station the next morning to have his car checked for a long trip. When the attendant tells him that it will not hold gas, water, or oil, Haze stubbornly asserts that it is such a good car that a "lightning bolt couldn't stop it!" Out on the highway, Haze is stopped by a policeman who discovers that he has no license. Observing that "Them that don't have a car, don't need a license," he pushes the ramshackle car over a steep embankment. It lands upside down, and the motor and various odd pieces roll some distance away. Seeing the car completely disemboweled, Haze is finally faced with the fact that it will not take him where he wants to go. He sits down on the edge of the embankment and gazes into space for a long time.

Haze's final revelation of his inability to see is brought about by the destruction of the car in which he had perversely and ridiculously placed his faith. That this revelation brings about a transformation in him is suggested in the similarity between the image of him sitting and staring into space and the final image of Enoch Emery who, after his transformation into a gorilla, also sat on a rock and stared into the distance. But what happens to Haze interiorly as a result of this revelation can only be deduced from his actions and from the effect he has on others, for beyond this point he is seen only from the outside.

After a long time Haze walks back to town, buys a

bucket and some lime, and returns to his rooming house. When asked by his landlady what he intends to do with it, he replies laconically, "Blind myself." He has apparently come to the conclusion that when he had eyes he could not see the truth of things, and has decided to destroy his physical sight in order to be able to "see." His self-blinding contains elements of penance for the blindness in which he walked when he had eyes (in this it resembles the blinding of Oedipus)[2]. It also is a literal expression of a desire for something "he couldn't get without being blind to everything else."

What exactly it is that Haze is now bent on achieving is not precisely specified. It is clear, however, that he has undergone a reversal. Earlier in the novel he had repeatedly asserted, "I AM clean," and had felt that his "cleanness" (his freedom from sin and guilt) depended on the nonexistence of Jesus: "If Jesus existed, I wouldn't be clean." After his self-blinding he says to his mystified landlady, "I ain't clean." His behavior suggests that he is no longer trying to deny the existence of Jesus and that, believing in him, Haze is indeed following him "off into the dark."

In the final chapter, Haze's existence is seen through the eyes of his landlady, Mrs. Flood. Some critics have objected to this change in the narrative point of view, seeing it as a flaw in the structure of the novel. However, in showing the end of Haze's story through the eyes of Mrs. Flood, O'Connor keeps the point of view rooted in the secular mentality of Taulkinham, and therefore maintains the unity of the novel's structure. Until his self-blinding Haze had consciously allied himself with a despiritualized and secular world, and this is the point of view reflected in the narrative. That world view continues to dominate the novel until the end, even though Haze has changed his allegiance and is (appropriately) seen as alien to that world.

Mrs. Flood is an example of the average sensual man (or woman) for whom good is equated with material comforts and pleasures. She has an insatiable appetite for the things of the world—"she couldn't look at anything steadily without wanting it"—and for creature comforts: "If she had been blind, she would have sat by the radio all day, eating cake and ice cream, and soaking her feet." Haze's behavior and his presence in her house constantly present her with a question: "What possible reason could a sane person have for not wanting to enjoy himself any more?"

Haze uses his government pension checks (he was wounded while in the army) to pay for his room and board, but he is indifferent to money or any kind of material comfort. He spends his time sitting silently on the porch or walking around the blocks adjacent to the house. To Mrs. Flood's way of seeing things, he "could have been dead and get all he got out of life but the exercise." Even more beyond her comprehension, Haze practices bodily mortifications; he walks with gravel and small stones in his shoes, and he sleeps with three strands of barbed wire wrapped around his chest. Mrs. Flood protests to him that such behavior is "not normal . . . it's something that people have quit doing—like boiling in oil or being a saint or walling up cats."

The very fact that Mrs. Flood does not understand Haze's behavior, that he poses a continual question to her, makes her want to investigate him further. She begins to believe that he must see something she cannot, and she suffers anxiety over the possibility that "there might be something valuable hidden near her, something she couldn't see." Almost in spite of herself, her curiosity about Haze becomes an all-consuming interest that expands beyond any financial benefits she might get out of him. She changes her original plan to marry him (in order to get his pension checks) and have him committed to the state insane asylum; instead, she decides to marry him and keep him with her: "Watching his face had become a habit with her; she wanted to penetrate the darkness behind it and see for herself what was there."

Mrs. Flood visualizes the darkness of blindness in which Haze lives as a "dark tunnel." It is analogous to the darkness of death ("it occurred to her suddenly that when she was dead she would be blind too"). However, it is impossible for her to imagine the tunnel without imagining a "pin point of light" at the end of it; the point of light seems to her to be "some kind of a star, like the star on Christmas cards." Initially, the thought of Haze "going backwards to Bethlehem"—to the Christmas star—makes her laugh with derision. By the end of the novel, however, she has come to the conclusion that she wants Haze, not only for the material advantages she can get out of him, but as a guide for the regions of darkness, of the unknown, of death: "If she was going to be blind when she was dead, who better to guide her than a blind man?"

Mrs. Flood proposes marriage to Haze, offering him what he was searching for in the beginning of the novel: a home, a "place of [his] own to be." Haze, however, is no longer looking for a physical "place to be." He refuses her proposal by leaving her house. He has some destination in mind—"I want to go on where I'm going," are his last words in the novel. But physical destinations seem no longer to exist for him: "There's no other house," he says to her, "nor no other city." Two days later he is found half-conscious in a drainage ditch by two moronic policemen, one of whom hits him over the head with a billyclub to keep him from making any trouble. They bring him back, dead, to Mrs. Flood, who has him placed on her bed and sits down beside him to talk to him. "Well, Mr. Motes," she says, "I see you've come home!"

On the literal level, Haze's "homecoming" is a cruel irony, a sardonic twisting of the traditional way of ending a comedy (in homecoming, marriage, or the reunion of what was separated). Yet the imagery of the final paragraph suggests that another level of meaning is also present. Sitting beside Haze, Mrs. Flood stares into the "deep burned eye sockets [that] seemed to lead into the dark tunnel where he had disappeared." Unable to see anything, she shuts her eyes and sees "the pin point of light but so far away that she could not hold it steady in her mind." Finally, "staring with her eyes shut," she begins to see Haze "moving farther and farther away, farther and farther into the darkness until he was the pin point of light." That Haze becomes one with the point of light suggests that the novel does indeed end in a form of union, the marriage of Haze with light.

The novel moves from images of alienation, isolation, and imprisonment, to this final image of union. Haze's initial alienation from himself was expressed in the mechanical, alienated quality of his actions, which were charged with a strange intensity but were devoid of emotion or human feeling. Though he was aware of his alienation (this was expressed in the image of his need for a home), he was not aware of its real source, which was his alienation from God, the Ground of his being. He was convinced that "the misery he had was a longing for home; it had nothing to do with Jesus."

Haze also suffered from a sense of isolation and imprisonment. He identified what oppressed him as a feeling of confinement, and he identified confinement with death—with being enclosed in a coffin and buried. He was bent on avoiding death and finding a place to live, to "be," in the city. However, Taulkinham offered only more images of confinement: furnished rooms, animal cages at the zoo, the glass case in which the mummy was locked, and Haze's car (in which he slept one night and dreamed that he was "not dead but only buried"). The imagery associated with Haze earlier in the novel suggests that he was imprisoned in himself. When he was nervous, his heart began to "grip him like a little ape clutching the bars of its cage." In one of her more elaborate similes O'Connor compared his face to "one of those closet doors in gangster pictures where someone is tied to a chair behind it with a towel in his mouth."

At the end of the first chapter (in which most of the themes of the novel are established) O'Connor suggested the means to free Haze from his imprisonment: Jesus. Haze, confined in his coffinlike berth, had awakened and cried out, "I can't be closed up in this thing. Get me out!" When the porter, who was watching him, did not respond, Haze repeated in a profane way the name of Jesus. On the literal level Haze's profanity is another instance of the profanity that frequently flows from the mouths of Haze and other characters. However, O'Connor characteristically plays on the literal meaning of language that is empty of meaning in the context in which it is spoken. For instance, the fake blind preacher, Hawks, said to Haze, "you can't run away from Jesus. Jesus is a fact." Hawks is not true, and the reader perceives that in his mouth the words are empty. Yet the novel shows that Haze, indeed, cannot run away from Jesus. When Haze blasphemes, the very presence of the name of Jesus—in the context of Haze's cry to be freed from confinement and death—contains the implicit suggestion that Jesus is the "answer" to his cry.

Yet Jesus is presented throughout the novel in such a way that he seems an unacceptable answer to the reader as well as to Haze. Because of this, some critics have tended to see Haze's dilemma in psychological terms, and to see his conception of Jesus as part of his problem rather than as the answer to it. The two strongly religious figures in Haze's family—his preacher grandfather and his grim and dissatisfied mother—are seen as the source of the warped version of Christianity from which Haze is not, despite ferocious efforts, able to free himself. His final surrender to Jesus and his death are seen as the results of his failure to escape from the effects of a pathological religious upbringing.

While one may read the novel in this way, one should remember that, in virtually all of O'Connor's work, two strongly opposing interpretations are possible. It is characteristic of her to create situations that can be interpreted in

two completely opposite ways, and to offset the theological
meaning she intends to be present in the story with a style
whose imagery, metaphors, and overall tone seem to suggest
an opposite meaning, or an insane or even demonic meaninglessness. The power that grows out of these oppositions is
considerable. While granting the power, some critics have
seen the oppositions as indications that O'Connor herself did
not really know what she was doing—that her conscious
intent to portray Haze as a "Christian *malgré lui*" was
undermined as it were behind her back by a subconscious
loathing for the world (or a secret partiality for the devil's
party) which expressed itself with great effectiveness in style
and metaphor. Thus Isaac Rosenfeld wrote of *Wise Blood*:

> It is quite clear what Miss O'Connor means to say . . . is . . .
> there is no escaping Christ. But the author's style, in my
> opinion, is inconsistent with this statement. Everything she says
> through image and metaphor has the meaning only of degenera-
> tion, and she writes of an insane world, peopled by monsters
> and submen.[3]

I would argue that the opposition between content and
style is conscious and deliberate. In placing Haze's story in a
context in which the imagery is often repulsive, even when it
is funny, O'Connor intended, I think, to arouse in the reader
a visceral as well as an intellectual awareness of the unpleasantly harrowing and unheroic and unromantic nature of
man's journey to God—a journey which, as a mythic, religious, or literary motif, is all too vulnerable to romanticization. The opposition between style and content creates a field
of irony, as it were, which makes any romanticization of
Haze's journey virtually impossible. It prevents the reader
sympathetic with O'Connor's religious position from too easily taking Haze's conversion as something conventionally
good and desirable, and forces such a reader to confront the
unattractiveness—even the frightfulness—of the "wild
ragged figure" of Jesus who pursues Haze. At the same time,

and from the opposite point of view, the emptiness and absurdity of the world of Taulkinham give, by contrast, a certain seriousness and power to Haze's religious commitment.

It seems to me that *Wise Blood* can be most fruitfully read if both the import of the style and of the content are given their full weight, and neither is seen as negating the other. *Wise Blood is* a mordant satire of varieties of religious perversion in an alienated world (and, simply as a work conveying the feeling of alienation and absurdity, the novel is impressive). But it is *also* a serious, funny, and paradox-laden account of the mysterious, compelling, and fearful attraction of the human soul for God.

5

•••

The Violent Bear It Away

Though very different in style from *Wise Blood*, Flannery O'Connor's second novel, *The Violent Bear It Away* (1960), has a similar subject: it deals with the unwillingness of a boy to accept the prophetic calling for which he was raised. The central part of the action in the present concerns his flight to the city, his ferocious attempts to resist his calling, and his ultimate capitulation to it. O'Connor's greater mastery of her craft is evident in the richer characterization and the complex interweaving of past and present in the later novel. While it presents some difficulties of interpretation, it is more accessible on first reading than is *Wise Blood*.

The action in the present begins with the death of the old prophet Mason Tarwater and the reluctance of his young great-nephew, Francis Marion Tarwater, to fulfill the old man's injunction to bury him ten feet deep and raise a cross over his grave. Interwoven with the present action is the history of the old man and the boy and their family. Old Tarwater was a prophet, a roaring, often outrageous mountain of a man who prophesied both when convenient and inconvenient. As a result of the immoderation of his prophesying he was once committed to an insane asylum, where he spent four years until he learned that "the way for him to get out was to stop prophesying on the ward." From this experience he "learned caution," and thereafter he "proceeded about the Lord's business like an experienced crook."

Old Tarwater had kidnapped his great-nephew as a baby from his only other living relative, his nephew George Rayber, and brought the child out to his clearing in the woods called Powderhead to raise him to be a prophet. Young Tarwater is the illegitimate son of Rayber's sister and an unstable divinity student. The sister died following an automobile accident, at the scene of which the child was born, and the divinity student shot himself afterward in an access of guilt.

Rayber, an agnostic, wanted to raise his nephew to live "in the real world" largely in order to undo vicariously what he felt were the crippling effects of old Tarwater's influence on himself. The old man had previously kidnapped Rayber from his agnostic parents when he was seven and had taken him out to Powderhead, baptized him, and "instructed him in the facts of his Redemption." For a few years Rayber had believed all old Tarwater had taught him. Then, disillusioned that the kingdom of heaven had not come and the world had not "blossomed into an eternal Powderhead," Rayber came to the conclusion that the old man had filled him with "unreality," and violently rejected both the old man and his teachings.

Rayber, in the company of a "welfare woman," made one attempt to get the child back from old Tarwater, at which time the old man shot him in the leg and in the ear (leaving Rayber with a permanent hearing impairment). Rayber later married the welfare woman, who left him after bearing him one child, an idiot named Bishop. Old Tarwater made several attempts to kidnap Bishop so that he could baptize him, but was unsuccessful. He has repeatedly told Tarwater that "[i]f by the time I die . . . I haven't got him baptized, it'll be up to you. It'll be the first mission the Lord sends you."

Tarwater is not interested in being the kind of prophet who is sent to baptize an idiot. He envisions himself a prophet in the grand style, striking water from a rock, as did

Moses, or commanding the sun to stand still, like Joshua. He expects to hear "the trumpet of the Lord God Almighty" calling him immediately after his great-uncle's death. Nothing spectacular happens, however. What does happen is that Tarwater begins to speak and think in a voice that is unfamiliar to him, "as if the death had changed him instead of his great-uncle." This voice gradually takes on more autonomy until it appears to be the voice of a "friendly stranger," who, though remaining an immaterial presence, is a definite personality, with a face "sharp and friendly and wise, shadowed under a stiff broad-brimmed panama hat."

Giving voice to the many thoughts the boy had been unable to fully express during the old man's lifetime, the stranger plays on Tarwater's desire to do what he pleases, now that there is "no hand uplifted" to hinder him. Taking advantage of Tarwater's unwillingness to dig a grave ten feet deep in soil that is "solid brick," the stranger reminds him that the agnostic Rayber, who is not hampered by ideas about the resurrection of the dead on the Day of Judgement, would burn the old man's body "in a minute" and save himself a lot of trouble. The stranger suggests that the old man's religious horror of having his body cremated is irrational, and that his desire to have the boy bury him in a way that is "suitable to his tastes" is just an example of an old man's selfishness:

His soul is off this mortal earth now and his body is not going to feel the pinch, of fire or anything else.

"It was the last day he was thinking of," Tarwater murmured.

Well now, the stranger said, don't you think any cross you set up in the year 1952 would be rotted out by the year the Day of Judgement comes in? Rotted to as much dust as his ashes if you reduced him to ashes? And lemme ast you this: What's God going to do with sailors drowned at sea that the fish have et and the fish that et them et by other fish and they et by yet others?

After questioning the validity of the old man's religious beliefs, the stranger begins to mock Tarwater's implicit acceptance of them:

If I burnt him, Tarwater said, it wouldn't be natural, it would be deliberate.

Oh I see, the stranger said. It ain't the Day of Judgement for him you're worried about. It's the Day of Judgement for you.

Similarly, he mocks Tarwater's expectation to be called to prophesy:

Look at the big prophet, the stranger jeered, and watched him from the shade of the speckled tree shadows. Lemme hear you prophesy something. The truth is the Lord ain't studying about you. You ain't entered His Head. . . . Anybody that's a prophet has got to have somebody to prophesy to. Unless you're just going to prophesy to yourself, he amended—or go baptize that dim-witted child, he added in a tone of high sarcasm.

In questioning the boy's prophetic calling, the stranger touches on Tarwater's desire for absolute freedom. Though the old man had repeatedly told the boy that he had kidnaped him from Rayber in order to save him "to be free, your own self," the old man's conception of freedom is not as free as Tarwater would have liked it to be. The old man linked freedom with baptism, and saw baptism as a descent into death from which one is "born again" into a new life ruled by Jesus. "You were born into bondage and baptized into freedom . . . into the death of the Lord Jesus Christ," the old man insisted to Tarwater. The boy, however, felt a sullen resentment that "his freedom had to be connected with Jesus and that Jesus had to be the Lord."

The stranger suggests that the old man's conception of freedom should not be taken too seriously because it was rooted in madness:

Or if he wasn't actually crazy, he was the same thing in a different way: he didn't have but one thing on his mind. He was a one-notion man. Jesus. Jesus this and Jesus that. Ain't you in all your fourteen years of supporting his foolishness fed up and sick to the roof of your mouth with Jesus? My Lord and Saviour, the stranger sighed, I am if you ain't.

Tarwater had been raised to believe that his freedom was limited to a free choice between Jesus and the devil. While he had no desire for Jesus, he had no wish to lose his soul to the devil. The stranger, however, assures him that "there ain't no such thing as a devil," and that the choice is "Jesus or *you*."

Finally, the stranger throws into question everything—secular as well as religious—that the old man taught Tarwater:

The trouble with you, I see, he concluded, is that you ain't got but just enough sense to believe every word he told you. . . . And how do you know the education he give you is true to the facts? Maybe he taught you a system of figures nobody else uses? How do you know that two added to two makes four? Four added to four makes eight? Maybe other people don't think so. How do you know if there was an Adam or if Jesus eased your situation any when he redeemed you? Or how do you know if He actually done it? Nothing but that old man's word and it ought to be obvious to you by now that he was crazy.

When a Negro neighbor comes to get a jug filled, Tarwater leaves the half-dug grave and goes off to the old man's still. His head is full of the stranger's jeers about a prophet making liquor for a living and bringing a baby "out into the backwoods to raise him right." When the stranger reminds him that the old man would "heat up like a coal stove to see you take a drop of liquor," Tarwater takes a swallow. Before long he has drunk himself unconscious. When he comes to, it is night. Unknown to him, the Negro neighbor has finished digging the grave, buried the old man, and gone away. Tarwater makes his way back to the house

(where he believes his great-uncle's body is still sitting) and
sets fire to it. He then sets out for the highway, where he
hitches a ride to the city and his uncle Rayber's house.

Outside Rayber's house Tarwater feels unpleasantly as
if he were "alone in the presence of an immense silent eye."
The silence of the night seems "palpable" and "waiting."

A mysterious dread filled him. His whole body felt hollow as if
he had been lifted like Habakkuk by the hair of his head, borne
swiftly through the night and set down in the place of his
mission.

When, having banged on the door and been admitted by
Rayber, Tarwater sees the child, his call to be a prophet
comes to him:

He did not look into the eyes of any fiery beast or see a burning
bush. He only knew, with a certainty sunk in despair, that he
was expected to baptize the child he saw and begin the life his
great-uncle had prepared him for. He knew that he was called
to be a prophet and that the ways of his prophecy would not be
remarkable. . . . He tried to shout, "NO!" but it was like trying to shout in his sleep. The sound was saturated in silence,
lost.

Tarwater's flight from Powderhead and his refusal of his
prophetic call end the first part of the novel. The comic tone
and natural imagery that dominated the scenes set in Powderhead give way to a much starker tone and to imagery of
inanimate (and often repulsive) things in the scenes in the
city. The focus of the novel shifts; with one short exception,
the action in Part Two is seen from the point of view of
Rayber.

A schoolteacher specializing in educational and psychological testing, Rayber has tried to compensate for the
"madness" he feels to be in his blood—inherited from old
Tarwater and awakened by his childhood encounter with
him—by living a life of spartan rationalism. Despite his
rejection of old Tarwater, however, Rayber has a deep (and

largely repressed) love for him, and "long[s] to have the old man's eyes—insane, fish-colored, violent with their impossible vision of a world transfigured—turn on him once again." When young Tarwater appears on his doorstep, Rayber sees the image of himself at fourteen (the age at which he first rejected old Tarwater) and sees the boy "engaged in a desperate heroic struggle to free himself from the old man's ghostly grasp." He recognizes that the boy "would go either his way or old Tarwater's and he was determined to save him for the better course."

A large part of Tarwater's motivation in going to the city is to find out what the truth is, his great-uncle's version of the way things are or the stranger's. He told the salesman who gave him a ride, "My great-uncle learnt me everything but first I have to find out how much of it is true." His behavior, accordingly, is guarded and wary. Despite the fact that he seems to claim identity with Rayber in announcing to him that "My great-uncle is dead and burnt, just like you would have burnt him yourself!" Tarwater retains a deep suspicion of Rayber. This suspicion grows out of the old man's stories of Rayber as a man who would try to make Tarwater into an abstraction, a "piece of information inside his head."

Rayber had once written a study of the old man—published in a "schoolteacher magazine"—in which he examined old Tarwater's conviction that he was a prophet and explained it in terms of insecurity: "He needed the assurance of a call, and so he called himself." The old man was convinced that Rayber would do the same thing to Tarwater: analyze him, explain his behavior in terms of conditioning and complexes, and thus deny the mysterious roots of his freedom.

Indeed, when Rayber is confronted with Tarwater, he does regard him as an object, as a "fascinating problem." He looks through "the actual insignificant boy before him to an image of him that he held fully developed in his mind."

Sensing Rayber's response, Tarwater hardens his expression "until it was a fortress wall to keep his thoughts from being exposed." Throughout his stay with Rayber he fiercely maintains that the old man has had no influence on him: "I only come to find out a few things and when I find them out, then I'm going." He rigidly resists Rayber's desire to help him and to transform him into the kind of person he, Rayber, would like him to be.

The surface action in Part Two deals with the conflict between Rayber and the boy that grows out of Rayber's attempts to "save" Tarwater from a "compulsion" to baptize Bishop, and Tarwater's insistence that he does not need to be saved by anybody, least of all by Rayber. Beneath the surface, however, both Rayber and Tarwater are engaged in a similar struggle to tear out the "seed" the old man planted in them. For both of them, the present reminder of the old man's influence on them is Bishop. The child, with his gray "fish-colored" eyes, resembles the old man physically. For Tarwater, Bishop is the object of the prophetic mission that Tarwater wants to refuse. For Rayber, the child embodies all that Rayber wants to resist—all that is irrational and inexplicable, and that cannot be used for some pragmatic purpose.

To Rayber's dismay, Bishop is capable of arousing in him an "outrageous" love that he considers "completely irrational and abnormal":

It was love without reason, love for something futureless, love that appeared to exist only to be itself, imperious and all demanding, the kind that would cause him to make a fool of himself in an instant.

Though Bishop arouses this love, Rayber feels that the child also provides a focus for it, and he fears that if anything should ever happen to Bishop, he would have to deal with an irrational love that had no focus and hence no limit: "Then the whole world would become his idiot child." Even with Bishop present, Rayber's "horrifying" love overflows Bishop and "like an avalanche cover[s] everything his reason hated." Accompanying it is the "longing" for the old man and his "vision of a world transfigured" that Rayber regards as "an undertow in his blood dragging him backwards to what he knew to be madness."

Tarwater, too, has irrational urges connected with Bishop that are associated with what he feels to be the threat of madness. Ever since his arrival in the city, Tarwater has been "engaged in a continual struggle with the silence" that he first encountered when he stood on Rayber's front porch. The silence seems to surround him "like an invisible country whose borders he was always on the edge of, always in danger of crossing." It demands that "he baptize the child and begin at once the life the old man had prepared him for." Bishop is so closely connected with the "silent coun-try" that Tarwater can see it reflected in the center of the child's eyes—and, as a result, Tarwater never looks lower than the top of Bishop's head "except by accident." Tar-water fears that if he gives in to the demand to baptize Bishop, he will enter into the silent country and "be lost in it forever."

So strong is the "temptation" to baptize the child that Tarwater "would have fallen but for the wise voice that sustained him—the stranger who had kept him company while he dug his uncle's grave." The stranger argues that the peculiar experiences Tarwater is undergoing—his sense of the mysterious silence and his inability to enjoy food, despite a persistent hunger—are only "sensations" and are not the sign of any supernatural call from the Lord. "If you are a prophet," the stranger tells him, "it's only right you should be treated like one." He suggests that Tarwater demand "an unmistakable sign, clear and suitable—water bursting forth from a rock, for instance, [or] fire sweeping down at [your] command." He insists that if Tarwater baptizes an idiot because of peculiar "sensations" he will be "confusing mad-ness with a mission" and will be "lost forever."

Tarwater has one very narrow escape from giving in to

the temptation to baptize Bishop when Rayber takes the boys through the city park en route to the museum of natural history. As they approach the center of the park, Tarwater begins to sense the presence of "mystery." They come to an open space in the center of the park in which there is a shallow concrete pool. In the center of the pool, water pours from the mouth of a stone lion. Bishop, who loves water, rushes to the pool and climbs in, and as he stands there the sun comes out from behind a cloud and rests "like a hand on the child's white head." Tarwater, in spite of his attempts to restrain himself, would have baptized the child had not Rayber understood what he was about to do and snatched Bishop out of the water at the last moment.

As a result of this incident Rayber concludes that old Tarwater has succeeded in transferring his fixation with baptizing Bishop to Tarwater and that nothing short of some shocking confrontation will cure him of it. Rayber decides to take Tarwater back to Powderhead in the hope that the sight of the burned shack and the half-dug grave would shock the boy so that his "irrational fears and impulses would burst out." Once Tarwater admits these "fears and impulses," Rayber feels, he can explain them to him, help him to understand them, and thus free him of them.

Under the guise of taking the boys on a fishing trip, Rayber brings them to the Cherokee Lodge near Powderhead. Tarwater sees the little lake on which the lodge is situated as another temptation to perform the baptism he is now more than ever determined not to do. The proximity of the body of water is so threatening to him that he comes to the conclusion that it is not enough to say no: " 'You got to do NO. . . . You got to show you're not going to do one thing by doing another.' " To prove to himself—and to Rayber— that he is not going to baptize Bishop, Tarwater takes the child out in a boat at night and drowns him. In the process of drowning Bishop, however, he also baptizes him. Though he does not intend to say them, the words of baptism ran "out of [his] mouth and spilled in the water."

In the lodge, Rayber hears the sounds of Bishop's bellowing and realizes intuitively what is happening. He exerts all his strength to feel no pain, fearing that, if he lets himself feel, he will be completely overcome by love, pain, and loss. He succeeds in feeling nothing. In so doing, O'Connor suggests, he succeeds finally in tearing up the "seed" the old man had planted in him. The seed is literally the message of the Gospel (see the parable of the sower, Mark 4:3–9, 14–20), but it is also linked with Rayber's capacity for love and for uncalculated emotional response. Had he not willed himself to feel nothing, his experience of Bishop's loss might have opened him to his repressed love for the old man and for the whole world. This love, O'Connor implies, may have been his salvation—his entry into the kingdom of heaven whose coming he had vainly awaited as a child.

The imagery of the closing paragraphs of Part Two suggests that Rayber has completed the dehumanizing transformation that began with his attempt to overcome the influence of old Tarwater by making himself as controlled and rational as possible. His partial dehumanization was symbolized in the hearing aid which made Tarwater ask Rayber flippantly, "What you wired for? ... Does your head light up?" After Bishop's drowning and Rayber's refusal to feel pain, the reference to the "dull mechanical beat of his heart" suggests that he has succeeded in transforming himself completely into a mechanical man. He has achieved the "nothing" he desired ("To feel nothing was peace," he had reflected earlier.) His story is finished.

Part Three focuses again on Tarwater who, after drowning Bishop, heads back to Powderhead "to live his life as he had elected it." He feels that in the week since his great-uncle's death "he had lived the lifetime of a man. It was as no boy that he returned. He returned tried in the fire of his refusal." O'Connor makes clear, however, that Tarwater's "refusal" is not bringing him the freedom to be himself that he believes he has won. Indeed, since he decided to drown Bishop, he has been losing significant symbols of his individuality. Though Tarwater himself seems unaware of it, he is undergoing a transformation into something resembling the kind of boy Rayber wanted him to be.

Initially, Tarwater fiercely resisted Rayber's way of looking at him and Rayber's view of life in general. He refused to give up the symbols of his defiant self—his country clothes, and especially his hat—and he refused to wear the new clothes Rayber bought for him. Similarly, he initially was unimpressed with Rayber. Gradually, however, as he came to see his refusal to surrender to the urge to baptize Bishop not as a refusal of a call of the Lord but as a refusal to take up the old man's madness, Tarwater began to accept Rayber's opinions—that the dead "won't rise again," that "you can't be born again."

Following his decision to drown Bishop, there was a visible and symbolic change in Tarwater's appearance. Rayber had taken Tarwater out on the lake in a boat, ostensibly to fish. He taxed Tarwater with being "just like" the old man and having "his future" before him. He stressed Tarwater's "need to be saved right here now from the old man and everything he stands for," and he proposed himself as Tarwater's savior. Tarwater expressed his refusal of Rayber's offices as savior by jamming his hat firmly on his head, taking off his shoes and overalls, and swimming back to shore. Rayber took advantage of his opportunity to get rid of Tarwater's overalls and plunged them into the lake.

When Rayber returned to the lodge he found Tarwater in the new clothes (except for his old hat) that Rayber had brought along for him: "In the plaid shirt and new blue trousers, he looked like a changeling, half his old self and half his new, already half the boy he would be when he was rehabilitated." Tarwater then accepted another gift that Rayber brought him as a "peace offering": a gimcrack corkscrew-bottleopener that Rayber bought at a filling station selling "false hands, imitation buck teeth, boxes of simulated dog dung to put on the rug, wooden plaques with cynical mottoes burnt on them." The bottleopener's association with these questionable items suggest that the wine of worldliness that it is symbolically intended to open is also an unpleasant and ersatz commodity. Though Tarwater disclaimed any use for the opener, he nevertheless accepted it.

After the drowning of Bishop, Tarwater adopts more of Rayber's values and opinions. He justifies his contention that his baptism of Bishop was meaningless because—echoing Rayber—"you can't be born again." To distract his mind from the thought of Bishop as he walks along the highway en route to Powderhead, he takes the opener from his pocket and begins "to admire it.... The little instrument glittered in the center of his palm as if it promised to open great things for him." He holds it "as if henceforth it would be his talisman."

How much Tarwater has lost the fierce individuality that characterized him earlier in the novel is suggested in his response to the suave young man in a panama hat and lavender shirt who gives him a ride on the last leg of his journey back to Powderhead. The young man's lavender eyes recall the violet-colored, hungry eyes with which the "friendly stranger" watched the drowning of Bishop. Tarwater senses "something familiar" about the appearance of the young man in the car, but he "could not place where he had seen him before." Tarwater proclaims to the young man that he is going home and that he is "in charge there now." He boasts of his independence: "Nobody tells me what to do." Nevertheless, Tarwater accepts a "special" cigarette (even though he does not want it) to disprove the young man's suggestion that "maybe you ain't had much experience smoking." He uses his corkscrew to open a bottle of "special" whiskey the young man offers him. Even though the whiskey is bitter and "burn[s] his throat savagely," he denies the young man's suggestion that he does not like it. "It's better than the Bread of Life!" Tarwater asserts vehemently.

Tarwater soon loses consciousness from the drugged whiskey, and is taken out into the woods by the young man and raped. As tokens of his conquest the young man takes away with him Tarwater's hat (the symbol of his old, defiant self) and the bottleopener (his new, Rayber-influenced self). Inasmuch as the young man resembles the friendly stranger whom Tarwater has come to regard as his mentor (O'Connor even refers to the young man as the "stranger"), his sexual possession of the boy, and his taking away these symbols of Tarwater's self, are an analogy for the friendly stranger's increased possession of Tarwater's mind and soul.

When he regains consciousness and realizes what has happened to him, Tarwater is horrified. He tries to purge the taint of evil from his surroundings by lighting a pine branch and setting fire to "every spot the stranger could have touched." His eyes, described as "scorched," suggest that he himself has undergone a fiery purgation. Through this experience with the young man who so resembles his mentor, Tarwater has learned that the friendly stranger is no friend but the very embodiment of evil.

When his friend's presence again manifests itself, Tarwater has made his way to the overlook above Powderhead and stands looking down at the clearing and at the blackened ground where the burned house had stood. The stranger's words indicate his covert possessiveness toward the boy:

Go down and take it, his friend whispered. It's ours. We've won it. Ever since you first begun to dig the grave, I've stood by you, never left your side, and now we can take it over together, just you and me. You're not ever going to be alone again.

Tarwater fiercely shakes himself free from the stranger's shadowy embrace, lights another pine branch, and fires the woods until he has made "a rising wall of fire between him and the grinning presence." He now regards the stranger as an "adversary" to combat with violence: "He glared through the flames and his spirits rose as he saw that his adversary would soon be consumed in a roaring blaze."

The tone and imagery of the account of Tarwater's return to the clearing emphasize that he is coming to a final encounter with the mysteries that he has resisted throughout the novel. The tone is quiet but intense, and the atmosphere becomes more charged as the final scene unfolds. His mysterious hunger "constrict[s] him anew" as he reaches the edge of the clearing. That this is not a physical hunger is emphasized when Tarwater, seeing the Negro neighbor Buford Munson across the cornfield, thinks he will go home with him and eat: "Instantly at the thought of food, he stopped and his muscles contracted with nausea." The connection between his hunger and the "silent country" is stressed:

He stood there and felt a crater opening inside him, and stretching out before him, surrounding him, he saw the clear grey spaces of that country where he had vowed never to set foot.

Tarwater moves across the field toward Munson. They meet with the old man's grave between them. When Tarwater finally lowers his eyes to it he sees, instead of the gaping hole he expected, a freshly mounded grave with a rough cross at its head. While Munson informs the boy that he buried the old man "while you were laid out drunk," Tarwater opens his clenched hands "as if he were dropping something he had been clutching all his life."

The imagery suggests that now, indeed, everything has been burnt out of him. His face is described as "spent," and nothing about him seems alive but his eyes. Those eyes, after his rape by the young man, had looked "as if, touched with a coal like the lips of the prophet, they would never be used for ordinary sights again." Now, his scorched eyes open on a vision. Lifting his eyes from the grave, he seems "to see something coming in the distance." The intensity of the atmosphere is too much for the Negro neighbor to bear, and

Munson turns and disappears into the woods. The empty field stretching before Tarwater comes to seem "no longer empty but peopled with a multitude."

The multitude resembles the one described in the Gospels when Jesus miraculously fed the crowd of five thousand with five loaves and two fishes. It also recalls the old man's image of heaven. He had told Tarwater that "as soon as he died, he would hasten to the banks of the Lake of Galilee to eat the loaves and fishes that the Lord had multiplied." Tarwater had been horrified at the prospect of eating the "bread of life" forever: "In the darkest, most private part of his soul, hanging upsidedown like a sleeping bat, was the certain, undeniable knowledge that he was not hungry for the bread of life." Moreover, he had sensed that this hunger for the bread of life, for Jesus, "was the heart of his great-uncle's madness." He had been afraid that "it might be passed down . . . and then he would be torn by hunger like the old man, the bottom split out of his stomach so that nothing would heal or fill it but the bread of life."

Throughout the novel, Tarwater persistently denied that he was hungry for the bread of life, despite the gnawing hunger that no physical food would appease. Now, in his vision of the multitude, he sees his great-uncle leaning forward, impatiently following the progress of the basket of miraculous bread toward him. Tarwater, too, leans forward, "aware at last of the object of his hunger, aware that it was the same as the old man's and that nothing on earth would fill him." Once he has accepted his hunger, he feels it "no longer as a pain but as a tide." The hunger has a motion, an energy, of its own; Tarwater feels it "building . . . rising and engulfing him." It seems to "lift and turn him." The "turning" is a symbol that a conversion (*convertere*, to turn) has been effected in him. His literal turning around brings him to face the treeline behind him, where the fires he set are still burning. These natural fires become the vehicle for a supernatural revelation: "a red-gold tree of fire ascended as if it would consume the darkness in one tremendous burst of flame. . . ."

He knew that this was the fire that had encircled Daniel, that had raised Elijah from the earth, that had spoken to Moses and would in the instant speak to him.

He receives his commission: "GO WARN THE CHILDREN OF GOD OF THE TERRIBLE SPEED OF MERCY." Smearing his forehead with a handful of dirt from his great-uncle's grave, he turns and moves across the field, beginning his journey back to "the dark city, where the children of God lay sleeping."

Tarwater's gesture of smearing his forehead with earth is rich in its implications. It suggests repentance, recalling the ashes smeared on the foreheads of penitents on Ash Wednesday, the beginning of Lent. It suggests Tarwater's willingness to enter into the sufferings of Christ, which are commemorated during the forty days of Lent. It suggests his acceptance of a vocation rooted in the realities of life on earth—the realities of humiliation, suffering, death—which he had heretofore feared and rejected. Symbolically he is identifying himself with the earth, as is emphasized in the description of the way he receives his commission: "The words were as silent as seeds opening one at a time in his blood." He has become fertile soil for the seeds of the Word to grow in.

Tarwater had earlier identified himself with the rigidity and impenetrability of rock when he boasted to Rayber that the seed of the old man's teaching "fell on rock and the wind carried it away." Tarwater's development is thus from unliving rock to living blood, from a thing that cannot suffer to a being that can. His acceptance of his commission is also the acceptance of the mystery to which, at the time of his first command to baptize Bishop, he had frantically said NO: the mystery that the Lord "had made him blood and nerve and mind, had made him to bleed and weep and think, and set him in a world of loss and fire all to baptize one idiot child that he need not have created in the first place and to cry out a gospel just as foolish." He has, in short, accepted the suffering and the incomprehensible mystery of human existence.

A common interpretative problem in *The Violent Bear It Away* concerns the question of freedom. Those who see the novel in a psychological light regard Tarwater's attempt to break away from the influence of his great-uncle as a movement toward freedom; such readers see his surrender at the end to the prophetic calling for which the old man raised him as a failure to achieve his independence. Even for some readers who are willing to accept the idea of a prophetic call as a valid religious option, Tarwater's apparent inability to say no to it, despite the most violent efforts, seems to suggest that he does not really possess free will. However, it seems to me that the novel is about two individuals with free will struggling with an inborn attraction toward the Holy; one (Rayber) resists it to the end, the other (Tarwater) ultimately surrenders to it.

O'Connor resists presenting the Holy in a way that is attractive, or perhaps even understandable, to the secular reader. It is presented as a mystery; it is suggested in the mysterious silence that surrounds Tarwater on the doorstep of Rayber's house, in the "silent country" he fears he will be lost in if he gives in to the urge to baptize Bishop, in Bishop's "silent serene eyes." It is linked with what is violent and irrational, with the old man and his prophetic frenzies, with the "outrageous" love that overcomes Rayber when he looks too long at Bishop or "at any real thing" (as opposed to the abstractions to which he tries to reduce reality in all its mystery). The mystery exerts a compelling attraction on both Rayber and Tarwater, and yet both are afraid of it.

This mystery corresponds to what Otto Rank, theologian and historian of comparative religions, calls the "numinous basis and background to religion."[1] According to

Rank, the rational contents of religion (dogma, ethics, qualities attributed to God such as love, mercy, anger, etc.) belong to the human or natural level, but the actual experience
of God on which these concepts are based is of another
order entirely. This other order Rank calls the realm of the
"numinous" (from the Latin *numen*, a god). It arouses in
the man who comes in contact with it a feeling of overwhelming awe and dread. It seems to me that Rayber's and
Tarwater's behavior clearly reflects human dread in the face
of the encounter with the numinous.

At the same time that it arouses in man the feeling of
dread, the numinous also exerts a compelling force of attraction upon him. Rank finds "only one appropriate expression" for describing the object of the numinous experience:
"mysterium tremendum et fascinans"[2]—a mystery terrifying
and fascinating. Thus Rayber's and especially Tarwater's
difficulty in resisting the numinous is not due to a deficiency
of free will but is an indication of the power of the attraction of the mystery that confronts them.

The power of the numinous mystery and the violence
of Rayber's and Tarwater's reaction to it relate to the meaning of the title and epigraph O'Connor chose for the novel:
"From the days of John the Baptist until now, the Kingdom
of Heaven suffereth violence, and the violent bear it away"
(Matthew 11:12). John the Baptist was the precursor of
Jesus, and his mission was to announce that the kingdom of
heaven was at hand. Clear signs of the breakthrough of the
kingdom into the world began with the ministry of Jesus.
Rank equates the kingdom of heaven with the numinous
mysterium; with the coming of Jesus, therefore, the numinous became present to the world in an intensely more demanding way. The intensity of the presence of the kingdom
draws forth a comparable intensity—a violence, even—in
those who encounter it. Whether the violence is that of
impassioned resistance (like Rayber's) or singleminded
commitment (like Old Tarwater's throughout, and like

young Tarwater's at the end of the novel), it is a sign that
the numinous mysterium in all its aweful power has indeed
been encountered. The epigraph suggests that only those
who have truly been touched by the numinous are capable
of entering into the kingdom—an entrance that in itself
involves a capacity for violence, as is implied in the image of
"bearing the kingdom away" or "taking it by force."

In O'Connor's conception, the numinous is characteristically beyond—and often in opposition to—the world's
expectation of what God, or His works, ought to be like.
Jesus is described by the child evangelist in the novel as the
Word of God and as love. The world, the child preaches,
having been told that God was going to send a king, expected a king who would have a "golden fleece" for His bed,
"a thousand suns in a peacock's tail" for His sash, and a
mother who would "ride on a four-horned white beast and
use the sunset for a cape." But when Jesus came he was
born "on cold straw," and his mother was "plain as the
winter." The world did not want "Love [that] cuts like the
cold wind and the will of God [that] is plain as the winter."
Neither does Rayber want the irrational love for Bishop and
Old Tarwater that threatens to engulf him, nor does Tarwater want the will of God that would lead him "trudging
off into the distance in the bleeding stinking mad shadow of
Jesus, lost forever to his own inclinations."

The action of the Word of God is no easier to accept
than the manifestation of the love of God. "The Word of
God is a burning Word to burn you clean!" the child evangelist proclaims. This burning Word is often communicated
by means of violence and even of evil. (As O'Connor said
elsewhere, "the devil accomplishes a good deal of ground-
work that seems to be necessary before grace is effective."[3])
But the imagery of burning is associated with a painful
purgation that can, if accepted, lead to vision, to repentance,
and to full entry into the numinous kingdom.

The numinous remains, from a human point of view, a

locus of violence, aweful and ambiguous. Tarwater, at the end of the novel, "his face set toward the dark city" and his "singed eyes ... seem[ing] already to envision the fate that awaited him," is a stark and rather frightening figure. It is not surprising that critics have sometimes found his acceptance of his prophetic vocation more disturbing than reassuring.

Like *Wise Blood, The Violent Bear It Away* embodies a paradox in that its theological content is offset by a tone that begins in comedy and becomes increasingly dark, violent, and horrifying. In seeking to interpret the novel most commentators emphasize one or the other pole of the paradox. Those sympathetic with O'Connor's religious point of view tend to see the novel as a straightforward account of the making of a prophet. Others, who respond primarily to the tone of the novel, see it variously as an "ironic jape," or as a strident satire on the destructive power of religious obsession, or as a sinister vision of a world emptied of meaning in which both Rayber and Tarwater unsuccessfully fight "against their own pervasive feeling of nothingness." It seems to me, however, that to separate the tone from the content and to interpret the novel on the basis of one *or* the other is to lose the tension that gives the novel its power.

This tension grows out of the paradox that, while the story is indeed *about* Tarwater's encounter with the numinous mysterium, what Tarwater *does* arouses in the reader a mixture of shock, repulsion, and dread. This contradiction prevents us from seeing (and dismissing) Tarwater's ultimate acceptance of his prophetic call as anything conventionally "good." It also makes us uncomfortably aware of what is, to the human point of view, the extremity and exigency of the transcendent. It is thus a way of creating an objective correlative, as it were, of man's experience before the Infinite.

6

●●●

Conclusion

O'Connor's view of life and her understanding of what she was doing in her stories has occupied her interpreters to a degree unusual in modern criticism. Whether to explain her work in terms of her belief, or to show an alleged lack of connection between the two, commentators have had to deal with what O'Connor said and thought her work was all about. And somewhat surprisingly for a writer who was otherwise shy, she took good advantage of the opportunities she had to make her views known. In essays and in lectures given at colleges and writers' conferences, she repeatedly identified herself as a "writer with Christian concerns," a writer concerned with "ultimate mystery as we find it embodied in the concrete world of sense experience."[1]

Most commentators have explained her often difficult and provocative work by placing it in the context of the beliefs about life and art that she unambiguously stated in her lectures and essays. A small but important minority, holding fast to the canons of academic criticism, have maintained that her stories can be read and enjoyed solely as works of art, as "renderings and criticisms of human experience,"[2] without reference to the author's intent or beliefs. But for the most part readers and critics alike have been unable to ignore O'Connor's view of the world, and many have found it an obstacle very difficult to circumnavigate successfully.

This, I think, is exactly what Flannery O'Connor would have wished. While she was an artist of the highest caliber, she thought of herself as a prophet, and her art was the medium for her prophetic message. It was her intention that her stories should shock, that they should bring the reader to encounter a vision he could face only with difficulty or with outright repugnance. And she wanted her vision not only to be seen for what it was but to be taken seriously. She was confident enough of her artistic powers to believe this would happen, even if it took fifty or a hundred years.

Certainly recognition of O'Connor as a writer has not taken anything like the time she was prepared to wait. Between 1966 and 1974 more than a dozen books on her work have appeared, and a significant accumulation of critical essays has been growing since 1958. She is unquestionably being seen as a writer of importance, despite the fact that the body of her work is very small. Nevertheless, there is still a great deal of tension between her prophetic stance and the mood of the contemporary literary world. Of the book-length critical studies on her work, the two that were pronounced "best" or "most persuasive" at the time of their publication both repudiated the importance of taking seriously O'Connor's prophetic vision. One (Josephine Hendin's *The World of Flannery O'Connor*) denies altogether its relevance to the understanding of her work. The other (Martha Stephens's *The Question of Flannery O'Connor*) wonders if Miss O'Connor is one of those writers "whose private vision of things we respect less and less the better we understand it."[3]

Yet it is in the nature of the prophetic vision that it should be unattractive, if not unacceptable, to those to whom it is addressed. This is a fact that should not be lost sight of in reading O'Connor, regardless of whether one accepts or rejects her vision. Indeed, a too-facile acceptance of her world view as truth can be just as much an avoidance of the full harshness of her vision as a complete rejection of it. She wanted to shock the reader into a recognition that those blind and distorted faces in her stories are a true reflection of his own, and if the revelation is not as illuminating to him as the revelation that typically ends the stories is to her characters, one wonders if the recognition has truly been made.

Perhaps because of the harshness of her vision, her utter lack of sentimentality, and her persistent irony, readers often feel that there is little that is beautiful in O'Connor's work. Critics such as Josephine Hendin and Martha Stephens have picked out her less appetizing descriptions of people and things and concluded from these that her attitude toward the created universe was predominantly one of disgust and revulsion. Yet surely no one whose hobby was raising peacocks would be indifferent to the beauty of the created universe, even though, it is true, O'Connor's enjoyment of her majestic birds included an unusual appreciation of their less aesthetic qualities: their piercing cry, their penchant for eating her mother's flowers, their inclination to perch on gates, which sagged diagonally under the birds' weight. O'Connor's appreciation of the peacocks' nuisance value as well as their splendor is in significant contrast to what she believed to be a widespread human response to the created universe. This common attitude, evident in many of her characters, is that the natural world has no legitimate function other than to serve the practical needs of man. Her repeated presentation of the natural world as unsubdued and embodying some mysterious power beyond human manipulation is an indication of her own feelings about nature. She does not, as Martha Stephens contends, hate the natural world. Rather, she sees it as a manifestation of divine power, and both its austere beauty and its indifference to the pragmatic concerns of men are signs of its relationship to the divine.

To see the beauty of O'Connor's work, one should consider the work as a whole: the economy and clarity of the imagery, the design and structure of the stories, and that indefinable quality Thomas Aquinas calls "radiance," which stems more from the perfection of the artist's work than from its evocation of what is conventionally understood to be beautiful. It seems clear that O'Connor felt that beauty—like the concept of good—had been sentimentalized into mere prettiness and social acceptability. Her own view of the matter, I would deduce, is that beauty is consubstantial with truth, and that truth, with all its depth and severity, is experienced as beautiful to the degree that it is accurately perceived and appreciated. O'Connor's characteristically unsmiling poses for photographers, for instance, or her fierce portrait of herself holding a peacock, suggest her unwillingness to betray the truth of what she was with conventional smiles and poses.

O'Connor's beauty was in her work, in her fidelity to her vocation as a writer, which was also a fidelity to the truth of herself, to her uniqueness, and to her special gifts. Theodore Solotaroff called her "a major writer, who . . . achieved a mastery of form and an austere strength of moral vision."[4] Thomas Merton[5] compared her to Sophocles, Thomas Carlson[6] to Aeschylus. For a writer of our own times to be placed in such august company is almost too much; we feel the judgement must be premature. Yet I must acknowledge my own response when I read O'Connor's work for the first time. I had sat down with *Everything That Rises Must Converge*, and before I had read very far I was overcome with the awareness that I was in the presence of a master.

Notes

CHAPTER 1

1. O'Connor, Flannery. *Mystery and Manners*, 1969, p. 33.
2. Ibid., p. 41.
3. Ibid., p. 226.
4. Ibid., p. 59.
5. Ibid., p. 44.
6. Quoted in Chase, Richard, *The American Novel and Its Tradition*, 1957, p. 25.
7. Muller, Gilbert. *Nightmares and Visions*, 1972, p. 5.
8. O'Connor, *Mystery and Manners*, p. 4.
9. Stephens, Martha. *The Question of Flannery O'Connor*, 1974, p. 3.
10. O'Connor, *Mystery and Manners*, p. 124.
11. Mullins, C. Ross, Jr. "Flannery O'Connor: An Interview." *Jubilee* 11 (June 1963), p. 35.
12. With one exception ("A Stroke of Good Fortune") the stories O'Connor wrote before her illness were not collected during her lifetime. They are included in the posthumously published *Flannery O'Connor: The Complete Stories* (1971).
13. O'Connor, *Mystery and Manners*, p. 132.
14. Fitzgerald, Robert, introduction to *Everything That Rises Must Converge*, 1965, p. xxiv.
15. Gilman, Richard. "On Flannery O'Connor." *The New York Review of Books*, Aug. 21, 1969, p. 25.
16. O'Connor, *Mystery and Manners*, p. 32.

CHAPTER 2

1. An exception to this is "The Artificial Nigger," in which O'Connor allowed herself, for thematic purposes, some beautifully textured descriptive passages. However, even here she tempered the serious and elevated style by irony; the "magical moonlight" which makes the floorboards the "color of silver" and the pillow ticking into "brocade" is, after all, shining into a backwoods shack.
2. Stephens, Martha, *op. cit.*, pp. 8, 9.
3. Pearce, Richard. *Stages of the Clown*, p. 4.
4. O'Connor, *Mystery and Manners*, p. 111.
5. Ibid., pp. 111–112.
6. It seems obvious that, as Leon Driskell argues in *The Eternal Crossroads*, in adding such a substantial coda to this story and placing it at the end of the collection, O'Connor intended to make a thematic link between it and the title story.

CHAPTER 3

1. Hendin, Josephine. *The World of Flannery O'Connor*, 1970, p. 102.
2. Merton, Thomas. *Conjectures of a Guilty Bystander*, 1968 ed., p. 170.

CHAPTER 4

1. Orvell, Miles. *Invisible Parade*, 1972, p. 50.
2. Robert Fitzgerald reports that O'Connor read the Oedipus plays when she was working on *Wise Blood* and had "reached an impasse with Haze and didn't know how to finish him off." Haze's blinding is clearly indebted to the blinding of Oedipus. See Fitzgerald, introduction to *Everything That Rises Must Converge*, pp. xv–xvi.
3. Rosenfeld, Isaac. Review of *Wise Blood*. *New Republic*, July 7, 1952, p. 20.

CHAPTER 5

1. Rank, Otto. *The Idea of the Holy*, 1958 ed., p. 60.
2. Ibid., p. 12.
3. O'Connor, *Mystery and Manners*, p. 117.
4. Rank, *op. cit.*, p. 82.

CHAPTER 6

1. O'Connor, *Mystery and Manners*, p. 125.
2. Howe, Irving. Review of *Everything That Rises Must Converge* in *The New York Review of Books*, Sept. 30, 1965, p. 16.
3. Stephens, Martha, *op. cit.*, p. 37.
4. Solotaroff, Theodore. Review of *Everything That Rises Must Converge. Book Week*, May 30, 1965, p. 13.
5. Merton, Thomas. "Flannery O'Connor." *Jubilee* 12 (Nov. 1964), p. 53.
6. Carlson, Thomas. "Flannery O'Connor: The Manichaean Dilemma." *Sewanee Review*, vol. LXXVII, no. 2 (Spring 1969), p. 274.

Bibliography

1. WORKS BY FLANNERY O'CONNOR

Collected Stories. New York: Farrar, Straus and Giroux, 1971.

Everything That Rises Must Converge. New York: Farrar, Straus and Giroux, 1965.

A Good Man Is Hard To Find, and Other Stories. New York: Harcourt, Brace & Co., 1955.

Mystery and Manners, Occasional Prose, selected and edited by Sally and Robert Fitzgerald. New York: Farrar, Straus and Giroux, 1969.

The Violent Bear It Away. New York: Farrar, Straus and Cudahy, 1960.

Wise Blood. New York: Harcourt, Brace & Co., 1952.

2. BOOKS ABOUT FLANNERY O'CONNOR

Browning, Preston M. *Flannery O'Connor*. Carbondale: Southern Illinois University Press, 1974.

Drake, Robert. *Flannery O'Connor: A Critical Essay*. Contemporary Writers in Christian Perspective. William B. Eerdmans, Publisher, 1966.

Driskell, Leon, and Joan T. Brittain. *Eternal Crossroads: The Art of Flannery O'Connor*. Lexington: University Press of Kentucky, 1971.

Eggenschwiler, David. *The Christian Humanism of Flannery O'Connor*. Detroit: Wayne State University Press, 1972.

Feeley, Kathleen. *Flannery O'Connor: The Voice of the Pea-cock*. New Brunswick, New Jersey: Rutgers University Press, 1972.

Friedman, Melvin J., and Lewis A. Lawson, eds. *The Added Dimension: The Mind and Art of Flannery O'Connor*. New York: Fordham University Press, 1966.

Hendin, Josephine. *The World of Flannery O'Connor*. Bloomington: Indiana University Press, 1970.

Hyman, Stanley Edgar. *Flannery O'Connor*. University of Minnesota Pamphlets on American Writers, no. 54. Minneapolis: University of Minnesota Press, 1966.

Martin, Carter W. *The True Country. Themes in the Fiction of Flannery O'Connor*. Nashville: Vanderbilt University Press, 1969.

Muller, Gilbert. *Nightmares and Visions: Flannery O'Connor and the Catholic Grotesque*. Athens: University of Georgia Press, 1972.

Orvell, Miles. *Invisible Parade: The Fiction of Flannery O'Connor*. Philadelphia: Temple University Press, 1972.

Stephens, Martha. *The Question of Flannery O'Connor*. Baton Rouge: Louisiana State University Press, 1973.

Walters, Dorothy. *Flannery O'Connor*. Twayne Publishers, Inc., New York, 1973.

3. ARTICLES ON FLANNERY O'CONNOR

Asals, Frederick. "The Mythic Dimensions of Flannery O'Connor's 'Greenleaf,'" *Studies in Short Fiction*, Vol. V, no. 4 (Summer, 1968), pp. 317–330.

Browning, Preston M., Jr. "Flannery O'Connor and the Grotesque Recovery of the Holy," in Scott, Nathan A., Jr., editor, *Adversity and Grace: Studies in Recent American Literature* (Chicago: University of Chicago Press), 1968.

———. " 'Parker's Back': Flannery O'Connor's Iconography of Salvation by Profanity," *Studies in Short Fiction*, Vol. VI, no. 5 (Fall, 1969), pp. 525–35.

Burns, Stuart L. "Flannery O'Connor's *The Violent Bear It*

Away: Apotheosis in Failure," *Sewanee Review*, Vol. LXXVI, no. 2 (Spring, 1968), pp. 319–336.

Carlson, Thomas M. "Flannery O'Connor: The Manichaean Dilemma," *Sewanee Review*, Vol. LXXVII, no. 2 (Spring, 1969), pp. 254–76.

Cheney, Brainard. "Flannery O'Connor's Campaign for her Country," *Sewanee Review*, Vol. LXXII, no. 4 (Autumn, 1964), pp. 555–558.

Detweiler, Robert. "The Curse of Christ in Flannery O'Connor's Fiction," *Comparative Literature Studies*, Vol. III, no. 2 (1966), pp. 235–45.

Fitzgerald, Robert. "The Countryside and the True Country," *Sewanee Review*, Vol. LXX (1962), pp. 380–394.

Gilman, Richard. "On Flannery O'Connor," *New York Review of Books*, Aug. 21, 1969, pp. 24–26.

Gordon, Caroline. "Flannery O'Connor's *Wise Blood*," *Critique*, Vol. II (1958–59), pp. 3–10.

Hawkes, John. "Flannery O'Connor's Devil," *Sewanee Review*, Vol. LXX (1962), pp. 395–407.

Howe, Irving. Review of *Everything That Rises Must Converge*, *New York Review of Books*, Sept. 30, 1965, pp. 16–17.

Lorch, Thomas M. "Flannery O'Connor: Christian Allegorist," *Critique*, Vol. X, no. 2, pp. 69–80.

Montgomery, Marion. "Miss O'Connor and the Christ-Haunted," *Southern Review*, Vol. 4 (Summer, 1968), pp. 665–72.

———. "O'Connor and Teilhard de Chardin: The Problem of Evil," *Renascence*, Vol. XXII, no. 1 (Autumn 1969), pp. 34–42.

Muller, Gilbert H. "The City of Woe: Flannery O'Connor's Dantean Vision," *Georgia Review*, Vol. XXIII, no. 2 (Summer 1969), pp. 206–213.

Sullivan, Walter. "Flannery O'Connor, Sin and Grace: *Everything That Rises Must Converge*," *Hollins Critic*, Vol. II, no. 4 (Summer, 1965), pp. 1–8, 10.

Taylor, Henry. "The Halt Shall Be Gathered Together: Physical Deformity in the Fiction of Flannery O'Connor," *Western Humanities Review*, Vol. XXII, no. 4 (Autumn 1968), pp. 325–38.

Trowbridge, Clinton W. "The Symbolic Vision of Flannery O'Connor: Patterns of Imagery in *The Violent Bear It*

Away." *Sewanee Review*, Vol. LXXVI, no. 2 (Spring, 1968),
pp. 298–318.

Vande Kieft, Ruth M. "Judgment in the Fiction of Flannery
O'Connor," *Sewanee Review*, Vol. LXXVI, no. 2 (Spring,
1968), pp. 337–356.

Index

Absurd
elements of, 89
literature of the, 4
Aeschylus, comparison with, 116
Alienation theme
in "A Good Man Is Hard to Find," 18–19
in *Wise Blood*, 86, 89
Ambiguity, 14
in "A Late Encounter with the Enemy," 24
in *The Violent Bear It Away*, 111
American literature
and "romance" fiction, 3–4
and Southern literature, 3, 4, 11
Anthropocentric point of view, 15
Aquinas, Thomas (quoted), 116
"Artificial Nigger, The," 14, 29, 40
Asa Hawkes, 76, 80
Asbury, 47–48
Autobiographical elements, 10

Bald Soprano, The (Ionesco), 17
Baptism, in *The Violent Bear It Away*, 94, 99–100, 103, 107–108
Beauty, views on, 116
Beckett, Samuel, 16
Biblical allusions
in "Parker's Back," 65
in *The Violent Bear It Away*, 92–93, 96, 106, 107
Bishop, 92, 98, 99–101, 102, 103
Bizarre element, 1, 3
in *Wise Blood*, 73

Caricature, technique of, 1
Carlson, Thomas, 116
Cartoon, gift for, 1
"Catholic Novelist in the Protestant South, The," 11
Characterization, 1, 2–3, 5, 7, 13, 14, 15, 17, 29, 115
and convergence, 63–64
in "Everything That Rises Must Converge," 44, 46
of freaks, 19

125

Characterization (*cont'd*)
  in "Good Country People,"
    37
  in "Greenleaf," 48
  and mirror image, 81
  in *The Violent Bear It Away*,
    91
  in *Wise Blood*, 73–74
Chase, Richard, 4
Christ. *See* Jesus Christ
Cinematic elements, 73
"Circle in the Fire, A," 14, 29
Civil War, and the South, 2
Coleman, 67, 68, 69, 70, 71
Comedy, 15–16, 17
  classical, 16
  in "The Comforts of Home,"
    54
  in "The Displaced Person,"
    31
  in "The Enduring Chill," 47
  in "Everything That Rises
    Must Converge," 45
  in "Good Country People,"
    35
  in "A Good Man Is Hard to
    Find," 19, 22
  and horror, 41
  and language, 35
  in "The Life You Save May
    Be Your Own," 25
  modern, 16–17, 19
  in "Parker's Back," 65
  and religious imagery, 46
  in *The Violent Bear It Away*,
    96, 111
  in *Wise Blood*, 73
"Comforts of Home, The," 53–
    56

Contradictory elements, 41, 111
  in American experience, 3
  in American literature, 4
Convergence theme, 44, 45, 46,
    49, 50, 63
  in "The Comforts of Home,"
    53–54, 56
  in "Judgement Day," 67, 69,
    70, 71
  in "The Lame Shall Enter
    First," 57–58, 60
  in "View of the Woods," 51

Death, 15
  in "The Displaced Person,"
    31–32, 33, 35
  in "The Enduring Chill," 47
  in "Everything That Rises
    Must Converge," 46
  in "A Good Man Is Hard to
    Find," 22
  and grace, 20
  in "Judgement Day," 68, 71
  in "The Lame Shall Enter
    First," 57, 60
  in "The Late Encounter with
    the Enemy," 24
  in "A Stroke of Good
    Fortune," 22–23
  in "A View of the Woods,"
    53
  views on, 7, 8
  in *The Violent Bear It Away*,
    91, 94
  in *Wise Blood*, 74, 85
Description, 115
  and characters, 52–53
Devil, 53, 55, 60, 110

"Displaced Person, The," 15, 30–35, 40
Dreams
  in *The Violent Bear It Away*, 106
  in *Wise Blood*, 74
Driskell, Leon, 41

Emotional flatness, technique of, 1
Endings, of stories, 13, 15, 25, 67, 115
"Enduring Chill, The," 46–48
English novel, the, 4
Enoch Emery, 76, 77–80, 81, 82
Essays, 11, 113
Eternal Crossroads, The (Driskell), 41
"Everything That Rises Must Converge," 44–46
Everything That Rises Must Converge, 1, 11, 43–71
Evil, theme of, 56–57
  in "The Lame Shall Enter First," 59
  in "Revelation," 61
  in *The Violent Bear It Away*, 104
Eyes, and sight imagery, 70, 71, 76, 97, 98, 99, 103
  and blindness, 80, 83, 85

Faulkner, William, 4
"Fiction Writer and His Country, The," 11
Fitzgerald, Robert, 1, 8, 9, 11
Fitzgerald, Sally, 11
Francis Marion Tarwater, 91–111

Freaks, as characters, 3, 14, 19, 24, 28
  in "Good Country People," 36–37
  in "The Lame Shall Enter First," 57
  in "Revelation," 63
  in "A Temple of the Holy Ghost," 27–28, 40
  in *The Violent Bear It Away*, 92
Freedom theme, 94, 101, 108

George Poker Sash, 23, 24
George Rayber, 92, 93, 94, 96–103, 108
Georgia State College for Women, 6, 8
Gilman, Richard (quoted), 10–11
Good, concept of, 116
  in "A Good Man Is Hard to Find," 18
  in "The Lame Shall Enter First," 58, 59
  in "Revelation," 60, 61
  in *Wise Blood*, 83–84
"Good Country People," 14, 35–40
"Good Man Is Hard to Find, A," 9, 15, 17–22
Good Man Is Hard to Find, A, 11, 13–41
Grace, moment of, 20, 110
  in "Parker's Back," 66
  in "Revelation," 63
Grandmother, the, 17–19, 20–22
"Greenleaf," 7, 48–50

Grotesque, element of, 1–2, 3,
    11, 13, 14, 26, 41
  in American literature, 4
  and characters, 19, 27, 39
  and technique of grotesque,
    4–5
  in *Wise Blood*, 78, 84

Harry Ashfield, 15, 40
Hawthorne, Nathaniel, 1
  and romance, 3, 4
Hazel Motes, 73–77, 78–79,
    80–89
Hendin, Josephine, 114, 115
Hicks, Granville (quoted), 11
Home, theme of, 74, 75–76, 85
Hulga Hopewell, 14, 35, 36–40
Humor, 4, 5

Imagery, 13, 14, 115–16
  of blindness, 37, 40
  of the bull, 49, 50, 64
  of home, 68
  of imprisonment, 86, 87
  of isolation, 86
  in "The Late Encounter with
    the Enemy," 24
  of light, 62, 85–86
  natural, 49, 64, 96
  religious, 26, 28, 40, 46–47,
    47–48, 65
  in "Revelation," 62
  of rising, 58
  of the sun, 23–24, 28, 30, 51,
    62, 64, 66
  in *The Violent Bear It Away*,
    101, 105–106, 110
  in *Wise Blood*, 85–86, 88
  See also: Symbols

Imprisonment, imagery of, 86,
    87
Incongruity, theme of, 6–7, 15–
    16, 19, 37, 41
Insight, moment of, 20
Ionesco, Eugène, 16–17
Irony, use of, 13, 16, 41, 115
  in "The Displaced Person,"
    30, 34, 35
  in "Everything That Rises
    Must Converge," 44, 46
  in "Good Country People,"
    35, 39
  in "Greenleaf," 48
  in "The Life You Save May
    Be Your Own," 25
  in "A Stroke of Good For-
    tune," 22
  in *Wise Blood*, 85, 88
Isolation imagery, 86

James, Henry (quoted), 3
Jesus Christ, 28–29
  and the bull, 50
  and Christ-like characters,
    15, 34, 40, 66–67
  in "A Good Man Is Hard to
    Find," 40–41
  in "Parker's Back," 64, 65,
    66, 67
  and the peacock, 34, 35
  Otto Rank on, 109
  in *The Violent Bear It Away*,
    107
  in *Wise Blood*, 74–75, 76, 77,
    80, 81, 82, 83, 87
"Judgement Day," 67–71
Julian, 44–45, 46
Juxtaposition, 27

Kafka, Franz, 47

"Lame Shall Enter First, The,"
     56–60
Language, use of, 16–17, 35, 87
"Late Encounter with the
     Enemy, The," 22, 23–24
Lectures, 11, 113
"Life You Save May Be Your
     Own, The," 7, 9, 24–25
Lourdes, trip to, 10
Love, theme of
  in "Good Country People,"
     37, 38, 39
  in "The Lame Shall Enter
     First," 58, 60
  in *The Violent Bear It Away*,
     98, 101, 110
Lupus, 7

Manichaean sensibility, 25
Mason Tarwater, 7, 10, 91–96
Melville, Herman, 4
Merton, Thomas, 61, 116
Metaphor, use of
  in "Greenleaf," 49
  and rising, 44, 46
  in "A View of the Woods,"
     53
  in *Wise Blood*, 88
Miller, Henry, 5
Milton, John, 55
Misfit, the, 18, 19, 20–22, 40
Mr. Fortune, 51–53
Mr. Guizac, 15, 31, 32, 33, 34–
     35, 40
Mr. Shiftlet, 7, 14, 24–25
Mrs. Cope, 29

Mrs. Flood, 83–85
Mrs. McIntyre, 30, 31, 32–33,
     33–34, 35
Mrs. May, 7, 48–50
Mrs. Shortley, 30–32
Mrs. Turpin, 60–63, 67
Muller, Gilbert, 4
Mystery and Manners, 11
Mystery of life, theme of, 1, 5,
     14, 15, 17, 25, 113, 115
  in "A Good Man Is Hard to
     Find," 21–22
  in "Greenleaf," 49
  in "Revelation," 62
  in *The Violent Bear It Away*,
     100, 107, 108, 109
Mythological allusions, 48, 49,
     83

Names, use of, 37, 48, 52, 63
Naturalism, 27, 78
Negroes, portrayal of, 14, 17
  in "The Artificial Nigger,"
     29–30
  in "The Displaced Person,"
     31, 32
  in "The Enduring Chill," 47
  in "Everything That Rises
     Must Converge," 44, 45,
     46
  in "Judgement Day," 68, 69,
     70–71
  in "Revelation," 63
  in *The Violent Bear It Away*,
     95, 105
Norton, 57, 58, 59–60
Nothingness, theme of, 111
Novels, 11, 91

Numinous mysterium, 108–110,
        111. *See also*: Mystery of
        life, theme of

O'Connor, Edwin Francis
        (father), 5–6, 7
O'Connor, Flannery
    Catholicism of, 7, 8
    childhood of, 5–6
    death of, 12
    education of, 6, 8
    illness of, 7–8, 8–9, 10, 12
    literary reputation of, 11,
        114, 116
O'Connor, Regina Cline
        (mother), 5–6, 9
O. E. Parker, 64–66
Orvell, Miles, 73

Paradise Lost (Milton), 55
Paradox, element of, 26
    in "Revelation," 61
    in *The Violent Bear It Away*,
        111
    in *Wise Blood*, 89
"Parker's Back," 64–67
Parody, use of, in *Wise Blood*,
        74, 75, 81
Past, romanticization of, 23, 24
Peacocks
    in "The Displaced Person,"
        33–34
    in "Good Country People,"
        38
    raising of, 6, 9, 115, 116
    as symbol, 34, 35
    in *The Violent Bear It Away*,
        110
Pearce, Richard, 19, 21

Percy, Walker, 2
Phallic symbolism, 56
Pinter, Harold, 16–17
Platitudes, use of, 13–14
    in "Good Country People,"
        35, 36
    in "A Good Man Is Hard to
        Find," 18
    in *Wise Blood*, 74, 87
Point of view, 13, 15, 54
    in *The Violent Bear It Away*,
        96
    in *Wise Blood*, 83
Prizes and awards, 8
Puns, 25

*Question of Flannery O'Con-
        nor, The* (Stephens),
        114, 115

Racism, theme of, 60
Rank, Otto, on numinous mys-
        terium, 108–109
Reader, role of, 5
Realism, 1
Religious themes, 1–2, 3, 4, 5
    and allusions, 13, 65, 92–93,
        96, 106, 107
    and Christian doctrine, 1–2
    in "A Good Man Is Hard to
        Find," 20–21
    and imagery, 46–47, 48
    in "Judgement Day," 69, 71
    in "The Lame Shall Enter
        First," 58–59
    in "Parker's Back," 64–65,
        66, 67
    and Otto Rank on religion,
        109

in "Revelation," 62
in "A Temple of the Holy
    Ghost," 26, 27, 28
in *The Violent Bear It Away*,
    93, 94–95, 107, 108, 110,
    111
in *Wise Blood*, 74, 75, 76, 77,
    78, 80, 81, 83, 87, 88, 89
"Revelation," 60–63, 66, 67
Rising, imagery of, 63
in "The Lame Shall Enter
    First," 57–58, 60
in "Parker's Back," 67
"River, The," 15, 40
Romance fiction
techniques of, 4
tradition of, 1, 3–4
Rosenfeld, Isaac (quoted), 88
Ruby Hill, 22–23
Rufus Johnson, 57, 58, 59

Sabbath Lily, 76, 80, 81
Sally Poker Sash, 23, 24
Salvation, in *The Violent Bear
    It Away*, 101
Sarah Ham, 54, 55–56
Sarah Ruth Cates, 64, 65, 66, 67
Saratoga Springs, stay in, 8
Satire, 1, 23
in *The Violent Bear It Away*,
    111
in *Wise Blood*, 89
Sentimentality, lack of, 115, 116
Sexuality, 49, 50
in "The Comforts of Home,"
    54, 56
in *The Violent Bear It Away*,
    104

Sheppard, 56–60, 61
Short stories, 11
Similes, 86
Sin, original, 44, 56
Social values, 60, 62, 63
Solace Layfield, 81–82
Solotaroff, Theodore (quoted),
    116
"Some Aspects of the Grotesque
    in Southern Fiction," 11
Sophocles, comparison with,
    116
South, the
cult of the past in, 23
gothic novel of, 4, 11
literature of, 3
views on, 2–3
Stages of the Clown (Pearce),
    19
Stephens, Martha, 6, 114, 115
"Stroke of Good Fortune, A,"
    22–23
Style of writing, 13–17, 41,
    115–16
and content, opposition of, 88
in *Wise Blood*, 73, 88
Suffering, theme of, 15, 28–29
and Christ, 67, 107
in "Judgement Day," 67, 68
in *The Violent Bear It Away*,
    107
Supernatural element, 65
Symbols, 14
in "The Comforts of Home,"
    56
of deformity, 38, 58
in "The Displaced Person,"
    35
of the hog, 60–61, 62, 63

Symbols (*cont'd*)
  in "The Late Encounter with
      the Enemy," 24
  of the peacock, 34, 35
  of trees and woods, 29, 49,
      50, 64
  in *The Violent Bear It Away*,
      101–102, 103, 104, 106,
      107
  See also: Imagery

Tanner, 67–71
Technique of writing, 1, 5,
    15–17
Teilhard de Chardin, Pierre
    and the concept of evolution,
      43–44
  on "omega point," 69
"Temple of the Holy Ghost,
    A," 14, 26–28, 40
Themes, 18, 114
  in *Wise Blood*, 74, 87, 88
  See also: Convergence theme;
      Death; Evil, theme of;
      Freedom theme; Home,
      theme of; Incongruity,
      theme of; Love, theme
      of; Mystery of life, theme
      of; Religious themes;
      Suffering, theme of
Thomas, 54–56
Time, in *Wise Blood*, 91
Tone, 13
  of *The Violent Bear It Away*,
      105
  of *Wise Blood*, 88
Tragic element, 46

Transcendence, concept of, 14–
      15, 25, 26, 63–64
  in *The Violent Bear It Away*,
      111
Twain, Mark, 4

University of Iowa, 8

"View of the Woods, A," 51–
      53
Violence, 1, 15
  in American literature, 4
  in "The Comforts of Home,"
      55
  of endings, 67
  in "A Good Man Is Hard to
      Find," 19, 22
  in "Judgement Day," 70
  technique of, 5
  in *The Violent Bear It Away*,
      104–105, 109, 111
  in *Wise Blood*, 82
Violent Bear It Away, The, 11,
      91–111

Wise Blood, 9, 73–89
  setting of, 4–5
Wolfe, Thomas, 5
*World of Flannery O'Connor,
    The* (Hendin), 114, 115
World view, 4, 9, 25, 113, 114,
      115
  and man, views on, 7
  and meaninglessness, 88, 89
  in *Wise Blood*, 83

Yaddo writers' colony, 8